Girl's Guide to DIY fashion

Design & Sew 5 Complete Outfits

- Mood Boards
- Fashion Sketching
- Choosing Fabric
- Adding Style

RACHEL LOW

FunStitch STUDIO
an imprint of C&T Publishing

Publisher: Amy Marson

Creative Director: Gailen Runge

Art Director/Book Designer:
Kristy Zacharias

Editor: S. Michele Fry

Technical Editor: Alison M. Schmidt

Production Coordinator: Rue Flaherty

Production Editor: Katie Van Amburg

Style illustrations by Monica Lee and
instructional illustrations by
Tim Manibusan

Photo Assistant: Mary Peyton Peppo

Photography by Nissa Brehmer, unless
otherwise noted

Published by FunStitch Studio, an imprint of C&T Publishing, Inc., P.O. Box 1456, Lafayette, CA 94549

Library of Congress Cataloging-in-Publication Data

Low, Rachel, 1972-

Girl's guide to DIY fashion : design & sew 5 complete outfits : mood boards, fashion sketching, choosing fabric, adding style / Rachel Low.

   pages cm

ISBN 978-1-60705-995-0 (soft cover)

1. Sewing--Juvenile literature. 2. Dress accessories--Juvenile literature. 3. Dressmaking--Juvenile literature. 4. Fashion design--Juvenile literature. I. Title.

TT705.L588 2015

646.4--dc23

                    2014033383

Printed in China

10 9 8 7 6 5 4 3 2 1

Contents

Projects

ACKNOWLEDGMENTS

I am incredibly grateful to so many people who have been on this journey with me. I cannot tell you how lucky I am to have such supportive and loving family and friends. Thank you.

To my sister: Words cannot express how grateful I am to you—for being there when I did not think I could get this book done; for cheering me on to keep going in my many moments of doubt; and for being my go-to when I needed some editing, creative input, and encouragement. Most important, thank you for being more than a sister.

To my dad and Cindy: I would never have had the opportunity to write this book if you had not believed in me and encouraged me to take an idea on paper and make it real. I love you both!

To Hallie, Kim, Heidi, Meredith, Ari, Josie, Liz, Judi, and Emily: Thank you for being so patient and understanding when I repeatedly said I was too busy to get together and for being my cheerleaders. I am so proud to call you all my friends!

To my Pins & Needles team: I greatly appreciate all your support, hard work, and creativity.

To Monica: Not only are you an incredible friend, but you also helped bring my vision to life through your divine illustrations. You are one of a kind!

To Michael Miller, Riley Blake, and Robert Kaufman: Thanks for being so generous and providing all the amazing fabrics I used in the book.

To Ute: Thank you for your perfect patternmaking.

To the entire C&T Publishing team, especially Kristy, Michele, Nissa, Alison, and Roxane: Thank you for allowing me the opportunity to be an author and for helping me bring to life my passion for sewing, crafting, and DIY. I feel so lucky to be able to share my enthusiasm and expertise with young readers to encourage their creativity. Thank you for your guidance and your patience with me as a first-time author.

To all my students: You are my inspiration!

To Molly: Thank you for being my best friend and watching over Pins & Needles each day.

To Tamar: You helped give me the courage to open Pins & Needles and follow my dream.

And finally, to my mom: Thank you for always loving and supporting me. I only know how to stitch because of you! I know you are smiling and would be so proud of me!

Dedication

for my mom & my students

Introduction

HI, GIRLS! WELCOME!

I'm so glad you've decided to learn how to sew, craft, and bring your amazing creative ideas to life! When I was your age, I dreamed of being a fashion designer. I wanted to have my own accessory line based on a little black suede bag with a fabulous sparkly crown on the front that my grandma gave me. I created a notebook and drew the different shapes, colors, and prints I would offer. I hope you are just as excited about being creative and designing! I feel so lucky to be able to help you begin your stylishly creative journey.

I created this book and all the projects in it just for you. I was inspired by the students at my sewing and crafting boutique, Pins & Needles, in New York City. My students are all girls your age who love to sew, create, and style.

I divided the book into five outfits for different occasions: school, hanging with friends, parties, sleepovers, and summer—all the times that I know you love to put outfits together for. I also have a section where I show you how to create your own mood board and illustrate your designs.

The projects combine sewing machine, hand-sewing, and other DIY (do-it-yourself) techniques. If you're a new stitcher, I'll show you how to use the machine. You can also start with the projects that don't need a machine, such as Dynamite DIY Sneakers (page 78).

In this chapter, I share some important and helpful tips for making the projects in this book.

Remember, don't get hung up on making *perfect* seams—that takes lots of practice. I designed all the projects in the book to be fun. So have fun!

Happy stitching and creating!

xoxo   Rachel

P.S. Invite your friends to join you and share in the creating. I love sewing in a group!

FOR *Adults*

I designed this book with girls ages 7–14 in mind. I want it to be a guide to get them started sewing and crafting and, of course, being creative. Detailed instructions and accompanying photos take them step by step through using a sewing machine and other stitching and crafting tools to complete the projects. This will give your new stitcher the foundation to sew and make things. Most importantly, I want this book to inspire girls to express their personal creative style through the mood board exercises, through fashion illustration, and, of course, through how they individualize each project with their fabric and material choices. I share some important safety tips (page 34) to follow when using the sewing machine and tools and also stress that they should ask an adult for help when needed.

FOR *Girls*

Some things I want you to remember:

Be open.
This is all about exploring something new.

Be confident in your ideas.
You are a creative star!

Be patient. Everything takes practice and time.

Be careful. Always have an adult nearby to help you with any of the more challenging steps and when you are using certain tools.

Be imaginative. This is the time to really let your imagination go wild—there are no rules in sewing.

Be mindful. Take it slow—do not rush through your projects. It is not a race, and it is important to take the time to complete all the steps.

Be creative. All ideas are good ideas.

Be stylish. Give your project your own personal creative signature.

Be happy. Have fun!

Be YOU! Most important is to be YOU and be proud of what you are designing and making.

After I make something it is so cool that I can say I made this.
Skylar, 9

Things to Know

TOOLS AND SUPPLIES

Let's go over some of the basic sewing and crafting tools. This was one of my favorite parts of learning to sew—gathering my tools. You can decorate a shoebox or shipping box to keep all your basic sewing supplies in.

Use fabric scraps, cut-out pictures, drawings, buttons—anything you want!—to decorate your sewing box.

Basic Sewing Supplies

Pull together these basic sewing supplies so you have them on hand for each of the projects. For most of the projects, special materials and tools will be needed in addition to these basics.

★ Pins and pincushion

★ Tape measure / other measuring tools

★ Fabric and paper scissors

★ Seam ripper

★ Marking tool (such as FriXion high-lighters or chalk pens)

I love to sew because you can make it unique and call it your own.
Mary Margaret, 11

What the Basics Are

Sewing machine A basic sewing machine will work best. Work with a parent or other adult when you first start sewing on the machine. Use the fun and easy-to-understand drawings of a machine (page 12) to figure out what all the knobs and buttons do. Soon I will teach you how to use it.

Iron An iron is an important tool to have to flatten seams. Flat and pressed seams are a must in sewing. Make sure to grab an adult when you need to use the iron.

Measuring Tools You'll need a flexible measuring tape (measuring at least 60″) and a flat ruler (I keep a 6″ × 18″ one handy) for making straight lines.

Pins Straight pins with pearl heads are useful. Try the Collins colorful pearl-head pins.

Pincushion Traditionally, a pincushion is shaped like a tomato. Try making your own pincushion with extra scraps of fabric and some stuffing. Then you can make it any shape you want. Sew it either by machine or by hand. Make sure it is stuffed enough that the pins will stay in place.

Scissors Have two pairs, one for your fabric and one for paper.

Fabric marker or chalk You'll need marking tools to make important marks on your patterns, to trace, and more. I like to use Clover chalk pens and my favorite FriXion highlighters, which disappear when you iron them. Always test a fabric marker on a scrap to make sure it works on the fabric you have chosen for your project.

Hand-sewing needles Find ones that have big eyes, such as Singer large eye hand needles or John James self-threading needles. The big eyes make them easier to thread.

Thread Use an all-purpose sewing thread such as Mettler Metrosene. If you are sewing on a button or something that is a bit heavier, try a thicker thread, such as buttonhole thread.

Seam ripper This tool is used to take out stitches, and every sewist uses one. We all take out our stitches at one time or another.

Safety pins You will use these to thread elastic through waistbands.

Some of the Extras

Interfacing This is a special material that can be either sewn or fused (ironed on) to the wrong side of fabric to make it stiffer and stronger.

Elastic Elastic is available in different widths and materials. We will use it for waistbands. For most of the projects in the book we will use ½″–¾″ non-roll elastic (like Dritz Knit Non-Roll Elastic).

Glue gun This is one of my favorite tools. I use it to glue everything! I recommend using a low-heat one. This tool also gets hot, like the iron, so make sure you have an adult with you when using it.

Fusible web This is one of the most brilliant inventions—it's iron-on fabric adhesive that comes in sheets and in yardage. Use it to smoothly attach fabric or felt designs onto another fabric or piece of clothing. Choose one with paper on at least one side to make it easy to trace designs. If your fusible web has paper on both sides, see which side peels off easily—do *not* trace on that side. I like HeatnBond Ultrahold. It is a great no-sew option for putting two pieces of fabric together. Follow the instructions on the package, because some kinds need to be sewn down as well if you want to wash your designs.

Freezer paper Freezer paper is an alternative to fusible fabric adhesive for appliqué, but you will have to stitch the appliqué down. It's easy to find at your local grocery store or fabric shop. Iron the waxy side to the wrong side of your appliqué fabric. Draw your design on the dull side of the freezer paper, cut out the appliqué, and then peel away the paper. Pin, then iron it to the surface you want to appliqué. Secure the appliqué in place by stitching around all the edges.

Pattern paper You will need large paper to draw or trace some of your patterns on. Traditional pattern paper has markings showing square inches to help you create straight and accurate lines.

Other papers For this book, you'll need paper that's thin enough to see the original patterns underneath it. If you don't have pattern paper, you can also use sketch paper or kraft paper from a stationery store, tracing paper on rolls from an art supply store, or newsprint. If you're using an actual newspaper, just be careful no ink gets on your fabric. You can even try taping together sheets of printer or copier paper until it's big enough to draw or trace what you need.

Fabric glue Not all glue is fabric friendly. For some of the projects in the book you need glue that works well on cloth. I like Aleene's OK To Wash-It glue (which can be washed, just like it says) and Aleene's Fabric Fusion, which is great for gluing down rhinestones and gems.

Pinking shears These are scissors with a zigzag edge, used to cut fabric so the edge won't fray.

Tools for Fun Embellishment

Many of the projects in the book invite you to decorate. Use paint, rhinestones, buttons, and more. When you are using paint, markers, and glue, make sure to cover the area you are working on with newspaper or kraft paper to avoid a big mess.

Fabric paint Get paint that is designed to be used on fabrics and won't wash out. I like Textile Color or Dye-Na-Flow from Jacquard, or Tulip Soft Fabric Paint. Get creative with ordinary items that aren't paintbrushes, such as sponges, pencil erasers, and more. Of course, a standard paintbrush also works perfectly.

Fabric markers Markers are more precise than paint. You might need markers that are permanent on fabric. I like Zig Fabricolor fabric markers, which are permanent after ironing.

Rhinestones and studs These come in different sizes and shapes and can be applied with a special applicator or a hot glue gun. Some are even iron-on. Rhinestones and studs are the easiest way to add sparkle to a project.

Embroidery floss This is a thin cotton yarn used for embroidery and some hand sewing. It has multiple strands together so you can play around with how thick or thin your stitch is.

USING A SEWING MACHINE

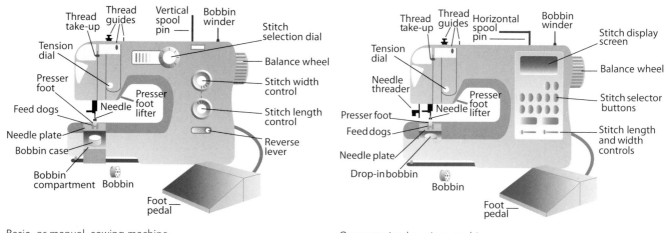

Basic, or manual, sewing machine

Computerized sewing machine

One of the most important and fun steps of learning to sew is getting to know your sewing machine. Look at the drawings (on page 12) and read about all the parts below. Use the manual to learn more about your machine, but if you get stuck, ask an adult to help you.

Know Your Sewing Machine

Bobbin It's a miniature spool. It holds your bottom thread—the thread below the needle. Wind a new bobbin for each different thread.

Bobbin case This is where the bobbin lives.

Balance wheel This raises and lowers your needle. Only turn it toward you.

Foot pedal It makes your machine go! Remember to press lightly to go slowly and keep control.

Stitch selector Use it to pick any of the stitches your machine can do.

Stitch length Pick how long or short the stitch is. The longer the stitch the looser the seam, and the shorter the stitch the stronger the seam. Stay in the middle (between 2 and 3). Some older machines list stitches per inch—you want 8–10 stitches per inch.

Stitch width Pick how wide your stitches are when using the zigzag or decorative stitches. Keep it at 0 for the straight stitch.

Tension dial It controls the balance of your top and bottom stitch. Don't play with this too much. If you have trouble adjusting it, call in an adult to help you.

Spool pin It holds the main spool of thread. Check your manual to see how to put the thread on the spool pin.

Presser foot This holds the fabric flat as it is fed through the machine and stitched. There are different feet for different purposes; your machine probably came with several. The projects in the book use the regular foot except when putting in a zipper. There's a foot for that.

Feed dogs Located over the bobbin and under the needle, these look like train tracks. They move the fabric under the presser foot when you sew.

Throat plate This covers the bobbin area and usually has lines marked on it to follow for seam allowances.

Getting Your Machine Ready to Go

Threading the Machine

Some machines have a threading diagram on them already. You can also look at the sewing machine manual to learn exactly how to thread your machine. Each machine is a little different, so these are general instructions.

Thread the machine from the spool pin through all the guides. Most machines have at least one guide on top, then the thread wraps around the front of the machine to the tension dial, take-up lever, and then another one or two thread guides before you thread the needle front to back. Unlike a hand-sewing needle, a sewing machine needle has the eye (hole) on the bottom (point).

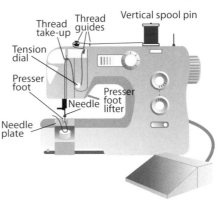

Thread take-up
Thread guides
Vertical spool pin
Tension dial
Presser foot
Presser foot lifter
Needle
Needle plate

TO HELP YOU REMEMBER

Stick small pieces of adhesive or washi tape on the machine to mark each step of threading. Label each piece of tape with a colorful Sharpie. This really helps when you are first learning to thread your machine. The tape won't leave any markings, and when you are a pro you can take it off.

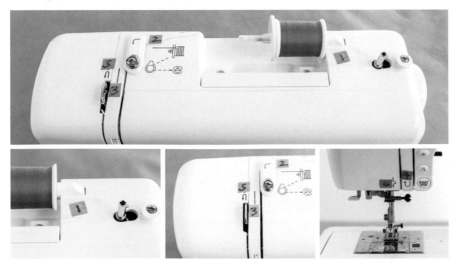

Winding the Bobbin

Put your spool of thread on the main spool pin with the thread coming toward you (or the way your manual says).

Pull the thread through the top thread guide like on the diagram (page 14) and then through the hole in the bobbin and wrap it around the center a few times. Place your bobbin on the bobbin winder and snap it into place. Then press the foot pedal until the bobbin is fully wound.

Follow your manual to put the filled bobbin correctly in the case (A).

Pick up the bobbin thread by turning the balance wheel a full circle toward you and pulling the thread until you see an extra loop of thread that looks like a little rabbit ear (B, C). Pull this thread out until the end of the thread is no longer in the bobbin case—now you should have two threads to pull and place toward the back of the machine and under the presser foot (D). Put the bobbin cover back on.

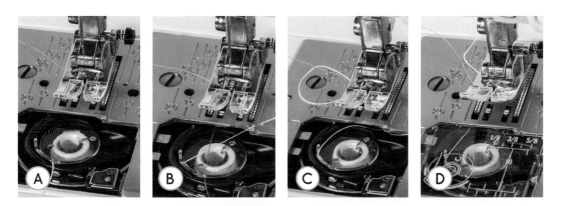

SEWING MACHINE NEEDLES

Sewing machine needles are different than hand-sewing needles because the hole is on the bottom of the sewing machine needle and the needle has a flat back above the point.

Make sure your machine is always threaded properly; always double-check that you have not forgotten any spots! You will know if you have when your seam comes out a bit wonky or your machine makes a funny noise.

Each time you finish sewing, pull the two threads (the one from the needle and the one from the bobbin) a few inches toward the back. Then when you are ready to sew your next seam the needle will not come unthreaded.

There are different types of needles for different types of fabric and thread. Check the needle package to help you choose the right kind.

Basic Hand Sewing

While most of the projects in the book use the sewing machine, some steps will require hand stitching, so here are some simple how-tos on the main stitches.

When sewing by hand, cut the thread you are using the length of your arm. Thread the needle, double the thread, and tie the two ends into one knot. If you are sewing something where the stitches will purposely show or are for decoration, or you simply want to use some heavier thread, try embroidery floss.

Let's practice. **Grab some fabric scraps and try each of these stitches.**

Running stitch This is the simplest of stitches and probably the most popular and commonly used. You pass the threaded needle in and out of the fabric in a line, making sure to keep the length and the space between the stitches the same. This stitch will come in handy when you sew in a zipper in the Necklace Dress (page 112), attach your appliqués in the Flirty Floral Cardigan (page 54), and more.

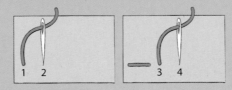

Whipstitch This is another basic stitch where you go over and under the edge of the fabric with your needle and thread. Try to keep the stitches looking the same as you go. You will use this stitch for the Hot Head Wrap (page 106).

Backstitch You bring the needle up (1) and back down to the left (2) to make a backward stitch. Come up again in front of the stitch a bit (3) and make another backward stitch that meets the first one (4). Do this over and over again (5, 6). You can use this stitch to write with thread.

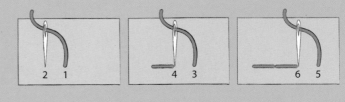

YOUR SEWING SPACE

I love to give the area I sew and craft in a little personality to keep me inspired. Sometimes I cover my wall with a mood board (see Mood Boards, page 22). I'll help you make one—or more (see My Mood Board, page 23). Sometimes just keeping piles of fabric and my stylish craft kit nearby does the trick. Make your space colorful and fun. Even if you're working on the kitchen table, you can cover it with some kraft paper and draw and write all over it.

Lighting and a comfortable chair are also important. Make sure you can see what you're doing. You don't want to have to squint or get too close. And you need a good chair to protect your back and muscles and to help you maintain good posture.

TIP Make sure to keep your sewing and crafting area tidy and all your tools organized. It's no fun to work in a mess.

Fun with Fabric

One of the best parts of designing and sewing is picking out materials, especially the fabric! There are so many different kinds to choose from—colors, prints, textures, and more. I love to use a little of one type of fabric and some of another. You can express your creative style with your fabric choices. Mix it up! Pair prints with solids, florals with stripes, or polka dots with something geometric.

Go to your local fabric or craft store and look at and feel the different kinds of fabrics available.

COTTONS

This is the type of fabric we will be using the most in this book. It is often referred to as quilting or crafting cotton and is available in many different weights. Most of the projects use light to medium weight, but for the sleepover tote and party purse projects you can experiment with some heavier or specialty fabrics. Cotton fabric is available in a wide range of colors and prints. Some even have special finishes—think sparkle or glitter!

KNITS

Many people say knit is not a fabric for the beginner sewist. I say let's give it a try anyway. Many of the fashionable clothes we love to wear—and thus will want to make—are made out of knits. Knits are just that—fabric that is knitted together, which gives it stretch. And all the threads are going in one direction.

Just like there are different kinds of cottons, there are different kinds of knits. Choose from jersey, interlock, and spandex. You can choose any of these for projects in the book that use knit fabrics.

Stitching with Knit

Sewing with knit takes patience and practice. If you do not use the right technique, the fabric will stretch and the thread will not. Also, you should use a needle meant for knits: these needles are called ballpoint or universal (these needles can also be used on fabrics that aren't knits).

Here are two ways to do it:

1. Use a sewing machine. Set your sewing machine to a zigzag stitch at a small length, between 1.5mm and 2mm. I call this the stretch stitch. You can also use a really small straight stitch.

Leave the fabric edges raw for a casual, unfinished look. If you want to finish the edges, use pinking shears to trim the seam allowances, or stitch along the edge with a zigzag stitch—not a hem, just a stitch on the edge! With some of the lighter-weight knits you can fold under the edge and topstitch. Try doing 2 rows of stitches to finish an edge to really prevent threads from breaking.

2. A serger is another option. It is a special sewing machine designed especially for knit fabric. If you have access to a serger, make sure to work with a grown-up to use it.

Some knits stretch two ways, others four ways. Most knits are made with Lycra. That is what is in any tights and leggings you own. It can stretch, but it also goes back to its original shape when it is not being stretched. The more Lycra, the stretchier the garment. Fabric that is all Lycra will stretch four ways. If Lycra is combined with other fabric it usually only stretches two ways. For the projects in the book that use knit, look for a combination of cotton and 10%–15% Lycra. Ask someone at the fabric store to help you.

WHAT'S IN YOUR CLOSET

I'm sure you have some things in your closet that you just don't wear. I know I do! Get those pieces out, and let's update them! In many of the projects in the book I show you how you can embellish and style an item you already own—such as a sweater, tights, sneakers, and a sweatshirt. If you prefer to start fresh then I suggest buying inexpensive, solid-colored items.

How to Use This Book

FINDING YOUR CREATIVE STYLE

What Inspires You?

We all have things we love, right? Clothes we love to wear, colors we love, music we love to hear. This chapter is all about sharing the things we love and expressing our love of those things. More specifically, the creative and stylish things. I call it discovering your *creative style*!

Creative style is all about what inspires you—color, fashion, television, music, books, websites, and even your friends. I am sure that for many of you *fashion* is on the top of your list. You may be asking: How do I know what my creative style is? The fun exercises on the following pages will help you figure it out. You can write everything down and make lists, but what is even more fun is creating a visual journal of your inspirations. Draw and doodle, cut and paste.

Exploring your creative style will not only be fun, it will also help you personalize the outfits you make using the book. It's all about putting your individual stamp on each project. Add a trim to the Double Layer Skirt (page 48), paint stripes on your sneakers, or draw a fashion collection you envision designing.

Doodle Pages

Find a sketchbook or notepad to doodle and draw the things that you love and that inspire you!

Mood Boards

A mood board is a visual journal that highlights or represents things that inspire you. Designers of all kinds create mood boards to document what inspires them or to guide their creativity when working on a particular project. Fashion designers make mood boards all the time, especially when they are designing a new collection. It helps tell a story.

I think of it as a giant collage! You can use magazine cut-outs of photos of what you like, fabric swatches, paint swatches, pretty tape or stickers, doodles you have drawn, pictures you have taken, and more. It can be just about anything that can be glued or pasted onto cardboard, foamcore, or a piece of paper. You can even create a mood board using a corkboard and hang it up in your bedroom.

Making mood boards was one of my favorite things to learn because I felt like I was a real designer working on an actual collection.

Laura, 12

A mood board can be big or small, and you don't have to create just one. Make as many as you like! Maybe make one that shows your inspiration for a fashion collection you want to design, another for a product you want to invent, and yet another for how you want to decorate your bedroom with all your favorite colors, music, styles—you name it! A food might even inspire you.

project:

My Mood Board

WHAT YOU NEED

I love to sew because it lets me express my creativity and imagination.

Hannah, 15

★ Colored pencils or markers

★ Assorted magazines and catalogs

★ Decorative paper to cut up (including paint chips from the paint store or hardware store, old cards, even cool wrapping paper)

★ Colorful and fun tapes and stickers

★ Glue or glue stick or double-stick tape (I like to use a glue stick because it is easy to apply.)

★ Large, sturdy piece of paper (like poster board), cardboard, foamcore, or corkboard

★ Selection of fabric scraps and trim (*Maybe* your local fabric store will cut some small pieces of fabrics— or *swatches*, as fashion designers call them—if you ask nicely.)

LET'S MAKE IT

1 Collect everything you would like to put on your board.

a. Go through the magazines and catalogs and cut out what excites you—a photo of a dress you like, or something that has your favorite color in it. You can also cut out words that stand out for you.

b. Look through your fabric and ribbon scraps and choose what fits your mood.

c. Cut up little pieces of the pretty papers.

d. Add souvenirs or pictures that make you feel good. Do you have a postcard from an exciting family trip? Or a photograph? Include that!

e. Draw something. Doodle. Scribble! Like I said, anything goes!

2 Organize what you collected on the board. Have fun with this step. You do not have to make everything straight. You can layer things on top of each other. For instance, put fabric swatches on top of magazine cutouts that you think complement one another.

3 Once everything is laid out as you like it, get gluing! Keep it neat; don't over-glue.

You're done! Isn't it exciting to put everything that inspires you together like that?

You can collect things over time. Cut pieces out as you see them and put them somewhere safe until you get ready to do your board.

MINI-MOOD BOARDS

You're going to have so many ideas and be inspired by so many things around you that you'll need a sketchbook. Any notebook will do—lines or no lines, it's up to you. This is a mini-mood board. Each page or chapter can be a new outfit, design, or idea. All the elements of your big mood board can be used here. (It's probably better to tape things or use a glue stick instead of white glue.) When you're ready to make an idea a reality, move the items or the entire page to a big mood board.

Pinterest Is a Mood Board

Another fun and creative way to make a mood board is to do it virtually! I know you spend lots of time on the computer, right? Well, the perfect complement to your mood board making is a fabulous website, Pinterest.com.

Pinterest allows you to create mood boards that live online in one place. This site is jam-packed with visuals of everything from fashion, accessories, and crafts to things for your room, party ideas, and more. If someone has thought about it or planned it, there's probably a board here. As you find what you like or items that inspire you, *pin* them (it's an icon you click on) to your very own board. Create separate boards based on your interests, and give each one a special name. Make one for each season, one for each of your favorite colors, one for all the things you like to do, and maybe one for all the DIY projects you want to make. All over the Web you will see photos that inspire you. Many will have the Pinterest pin button ready for you to click, so you can place it directly onto your Pinterest boards. Add things all the time!

IMPORTANT NOTE:

Make sure you have permission from your parents to use this site. You have to be at least 13 years old to use Pinterest, and many other websites. Always check with an adult whenever you sign up for any website!

HOW THE PROJECT PROCESS IS BROKEN DOWN

Each project in the book is divided up into three easy-to-understand sections: preparing, creating, and finishing.

Is This a Hard One or an Easy One?

You will have the answer to this question on the first page of the project. Find the adorable drawing of a tape measure; this is the guide to the skill level. The more inches shown, the harder it is. This is a little reminder that a tape measure is a must-have tool for any designer, from the beginning of the idea to completion of the project.

1"
Apprentice
total beginner

2"
Assistant Designer
intermediate

3"
Designer
advanced

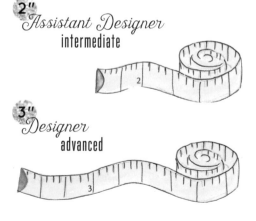

How to Prep

Before you start sewing or putting together your project, you will go through a few steps to prepare—gathering the tools, patterns, and materials you will need.

How to Create

Here you start bringing your project to life. This is when the magic starts to happen! The steps included in this stage might include machine sewing, hand sewing, using your glue gun, or maybe decorating with fabric paint.

How to Finish

This is like when you are running a race and getting close to the finish line—just a few more steps. You're going to stitch on buttons, hem, and embellish. Now's the time to make sure you've added at least a touch of your own style. Add some trim or ribbon, an extra bit of appliqué, or whatever creative thing you can think of!

How Do You Measure Up?

Let's get your measurements! This is one of the most important steps in sewing clothes. Do this before getting started. The chart at right shows the measurements you will need—bust, waist, hips, and distance from waist to knee. You will need to fill in the blanks. Grab your flexible tape measure and get measuring. Check the illustration to see where to put the tape measure—it might not be exactly where you think! This is the perfect step to do with a friend. It can be hard to get that waist-to-knee measurement. The number changes every time you bend over to see it!

Make a copy or two of this chart before you fill it in. If you are starting a new project and it has been a month or two since you measured, measure again. You are growing up!

Sizing

Patterns from different companies don't all fit the same. Compare your measurements to the size chart to pick the right size to sew for the book's projects.

Size	7	8	10	12	14
Bust/chest	28″	29″	30″	31″	32″
Waist	23″	23½″	24″	24½″	25″
Hips	29″	30″	31″	32″	33″
Armhole	5″	5½″	6″	6½″	7″
Waist to knee	18″	19″	20″	21″	22″
Waist to ankle	30″	31½″	33½″	34″	36¼″

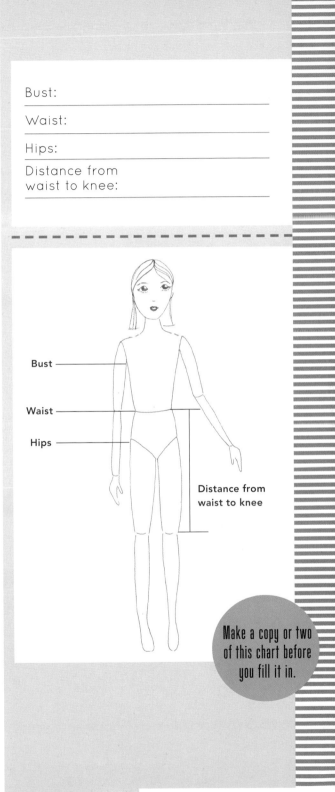

Bust: _____

Waist: _____

Hips: _____

Distance from
waist to knee:
_____

Bust

Waist

Hips

Distance from
waist to knee

Make a copy or two
of this chart before
you fill it in.

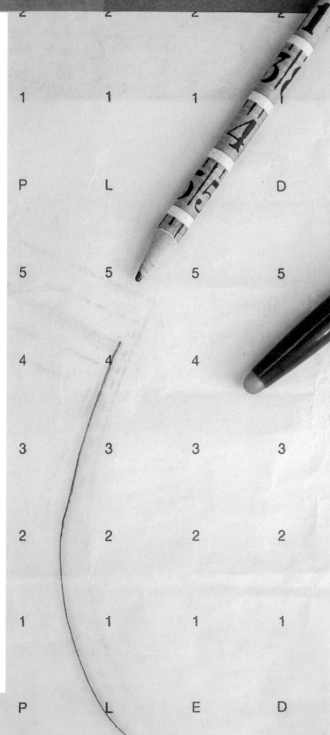

HOW TO USE PATTERNS

Working with patterns is an important part of sewing. For *most* of the projects in the book, you will use a pattern included on the pullout (pages P1–P4). Patterns provide you with the framework to cut the various shapes and parts for your project, whether it is a dress, pants, or an eye mask.

Some of the patterns overlap on the pullout or have multiple sizes in one pattern. You need to trace them first, because there may be another pattern printed on the other side, or you may want to make a different size later.

I like to trace all my patterns so that I can always reuse the pattern. You may want to make a different size later or use a different fabric. Or who knows? You may be wearing the dress you made and one of your friends might want you to make one for her!

Read over the suggestions for what to use for pattern paper (page 11) and get a sharp pencil for tracing. Any paper that's large enough and you can see through to trace will work. Try highlighting the original line you want to trace if it's hard to see. FriXion highlighters are great for this.

Label the pieces as you trace them, and include all the markings. On the patterns in this book, like all commercial patterns, there are various markings that tell you where to attach the pieces, where to place the zipper, or how to place the pattern on the fabric.

Making Your Pattern the Right Size

In your creative process, you may want to change things up a bit from the pattern. Keep this in mind when you are working on your Jeggings (page 68) and Peace Out Pajama Pants (page 82), to take them from cropped to long. Here are some basic ways to adjust the pattern.

Once you have everything traced, carefully cut out your pattern pieces. Keep everything organized and together so as not to lose anything.

Tracing and Templates

A few of the patterns included in the book are small enough that they can be traced onto copier paper or photocopied. If you are tracing, use thin white paper or traditional tracing paper. Trace the shape, cut it out, and trace around the cutout onto some heavier paper or cardboard. Cut this out to make what's called a template. It's easy to trace around the template to mark your design on your fabric. Now that it is on sturdier paper, save it and use it over and over.

★ **LENGTHEN**

Tape a piece of white kraft or pattern paper to the bottom edge of the cut pattern. Mark the new bottom and longer side lines with a pencil and flat ruler. Cut away any excess.

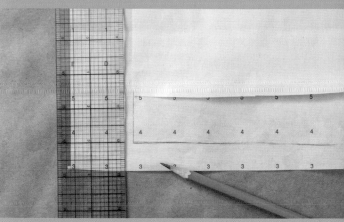

★ **SHORTEN**

Fold and tape up the pattern at the length you would like it to be.

Fold.

★ **NARROWER OR TIGHTER**

If you are in between pattern sizes, use the larger size and then make your seam allowance wider along the side seams to take up some extra space. It is easier to make something smaller than to make it bigger.

Important Pattern Symbols and Phrases

Cutting line

Shows you the size and where to cut. The patterns with multiple sizes have different kinds of lines for each size.

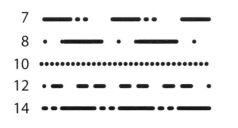

Place on fold

Shows that you need to place this pattern piece on the fold of the fabric—you will notice this on the Necklace Dress pattern.

Place on fold.

Grainline

Always runs parallel to (in line with) the selvage (see Selvage, page 33). Measure to make sure you line up your patterns on the grainline when you pin them to your fabric.

Grain

Notch

Tells where to match the different pattern pieces.

Seamline

Shows where you will sew. Not all patterns have this. If it's not marked, there will be instructions on the pattern to tell you what the seam allowance should be (see Seam Allowance, page 33).

Zipper position

Indicates where to sew the zipper into your project.

Organizing Your Patterns

Not only is it important to keep all your supplies and fabric organized, but you also need to make sure to organize your patterns. This way all that hard work that you've done—whether tracing a commercial pattern or making one from scratch—does not have to be repeated. It will be ready to work with again, too. If I love a skirt, top, dress, or accessory I made, I like to have it in another color or print. It's fun making my favorite things with all the different fabrics and materials available!

Pick up some basic file folders or large plastic sleeves at your local stationery store. Fold your patterns neatly and put them inside. Label the folder or sleeve with the pattern name and keep it in a drawer or file box or with your supplies.

I love to sew because you get to call it custom and you get to put your hard work into it.

Caroline, 9

Ready to Create!

SEWING WORDS

Throughout the book I will refer to a few terms that might be new to you, so here is what they mean.

Appliqué   A piece of fabric, felt, or trim that you cut into a shape that is then ironed or sewn onto another fabric (think of the word "apply") as a decoration. We will be doing a lot of decorating with our projects—it is one of the easiest ways to add your own personal *style*.

Backstitch   How you secure your seam. A special button will make your sewing machine sew backward when you press it while sewing (keeping your foot on the pedal). The machine sews back over your stitches; it's similar to tying a knot at the beginning and end of your stitches in hand sewing.

Right side and wrong side (of the fabric)
Did you know that there is a right and wrong side to fabric? The right side is the side that looks best—if you are using a printed fabric it is the side that the print stands out on—and the wrong side of the fabric is the dull side, where the pattern or color doesn't stand out. Most often we sew two pieces of fabric with their right sides facing. That way all the threads and raw edges of the fabric become hidden on the inside, leaving the outside nice and neat.

Seam   The line stitched when two pieces of fabric are sewn together.

Seam allowance   The distance between the cut edge of the fabric and the stitch line. For the projects in this book we recommend you create a ⅝″ seam allowance unless noted otherwise.

Selvage   The woven, uncut edge of the two parallel sides of the fabric. You need to know which edges these are when you get ready to lay out your patterns.

Scale   The size of something in relation to something else. A fabric print with big flowers has a large-scale design, and tiny flowers would be a small-scale design.

Stencil   A thin piece of paper or cardboard that has a specific design cut out of it so that when placed on the surface you are working with (your fabric, sneakers, sweatshirt), you can trace, color, or paint *inside* the cutout. For the projects in the book, you can use the patterns for letters and fun shapes to make your own stencils for painting.

Template   A copy of a pattern piece traced onto something sturdier, like plastic or cardboard, and then cut out. Usually, you trace *around the outside* of a template, so it's kind of like the opposite of a stencil.

Topstitch   When you sew on the right side of your fabric, ⅛″–¼″ from the edge of the fabric. We will use this stitch when we do hems on any of our projects. You also may use a top stitch as a decorative stitch, or to attach appliqués.

THINGS TO REMEMBER

Keeping it straight We try to sew our seams straight. It will become natural and easy with some practice. For a little help now, you can either line up the edge of your fabric with the edge of the presser foot or stick some colorful tape on the ½″ or ⅝″ measurement mark on the throat plate of your machine. Place the tape according to the seam allowance you want for your project. As you sew, keep the fabric lined up with the tape.

Rules for HOT Tools

Make sure you have permission from an adult to use these kinds of tools.

Iron Always keep your fingers away from the hot bottom at all times. Use the iron on a surface that is designed for the heat—an ironing board or pad. Make sure that you use it on fabric that can be ironed; some fabrics cannot handle the heat. Match the heat setting on the iron to your fabric. Don't leave your iron face-down. It can burn the ironing board and your fabric!

Glue gun Keep your fingers away from the tip. Do not touch the glue until it dries. Don't forget to unplug the glue gun when you are finished.

Pinning

Pinning is a big deal in sewing. You pin your patterns and pin to sew.

When you pin a pattern onto fabric, you always want the pins to line up and follow the edge of the pattern.

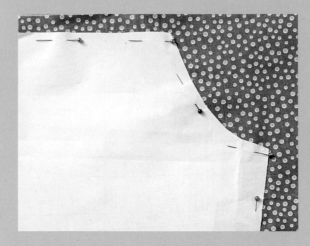

When you pin to sew, put the pins through both layers of fabric from the outside edge in to the center of the fabric.

Make sure to keep your pincushion near your machine. As you sew, you will take the pins out before the needle gets to them and put them right into the pincushion.

FINISHING TOUCHES

How to Hem

We are all different heights, and some of us have shorter legs or longer arms. So knowing how to hem will come in handy with almost any piece of clothing you sew—a dress, a skirt, pants, a shirt, and even your sleeves.

You will come back to these steps for a handful of projects in the book, including the Jeggings and Necklace Dress.

(1) Decide where you want your garment to hit. If it's pants, do you want them to end above your ankles or the top of your foot? Mark the garment at that spot and add 1½˝ to it. Mark there too. Now cut off the extra fabric—all the fabric below that 1½˝ mark.

(2) Fold and press ½˝ along the bottom edge to the wrong side of your fabric. Then fold it again toward the wrong side 1˝ and press again. Then pin in place.

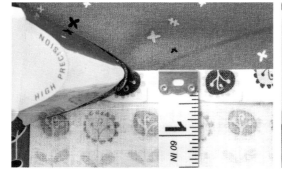

(3) Topstitch (page 33) in place. You can get creative here and use a different-colored thread as a fun touch! Use the edge of the presser foot as a guide to keep things straight.

Creating a Casing

Many of the projects in the book have elastic waistbands. Here is a quick how-to on creating what is called a casing—I sometimes call it a tunnel—for the elastic. The project directions will tell you to come back to this section to see how to finish your waistbands.

(1) Fold the fabric over 1½″ to the wrong side where the waistband will be. Pin along the folded edge.

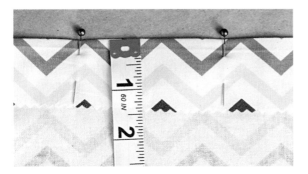

(2) Mark a 2″ space to leave unsewn on the back of the project, a few inches away from the back seam. This opening is where you will thread the elastic through.

(3) Starting at the mark, sew all around the inner edge, leaving enough space between the seam and the fold for the elastic. Backstitch at the beginning and again at the end when you get back to the mark.

(4) Attach a large safety pin to an end of the elastic. Pin the other end of the elastic to the top of the garment at the casing opening so it won't get pulled too far.

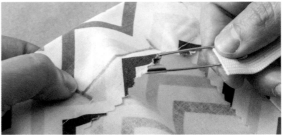

(5) Using the safety pin, push the elastic into the opening and work it through the tunnel. Be patient and ask an adult if you need help. A good way to think about it is to push, push, and then pull. You will notice some bunching, which is OK. Push until the safety pin is back at the opening, and pull it out a little bit.

(6) Unpin the elastic, overlap the ends about 1″, and pin them together. Check that the elastic is not twisted inside the tunnel. You can try the pants or skirt on now, and adjust the elastic if you want it tighter or looser. Sew the ends of the elastic together using a wide zigzag stitch.

(7) Sew the opening you left in the casing closed with a straight stitch. Remember to backstitch at the beginning and the end.

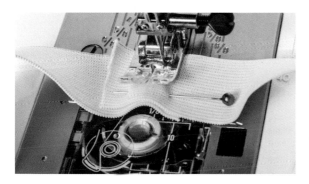

Buttons

I love buttons! I like to use them for embellishments as well as closures. So when you are thinking about how to decorate and style some of the projects in the book, don't forget about buttons. Here are the steps to sew on a button.

(1) Place the button where you want it and poke your threaded needle (use buttonhole thread or embroidery floss) through the wrong side of the fabric, up through the fabric, and then through a hole in the button.

(2) Poke the needle back down through the hole either next to or diagonally across from the first hole and through the fabric. Repeat through all the holes until the button feels secure.

(3) End your stitching with the thread and needle coming through the wrong side of the fabric and tie a knot close to the fabric.

TIP   To really secure the button in place, before coming through the fabric after inserting the needle in the last hole, wrap the thread around the stitches underneath the button and then go back down through the fabric and finish with a knot.

Zippers

Many of the projects in the book require a zipper. While I like all zippers, my favorites are the invisible zippers. They do the job, but you cannot see them!

Zippers come in many different lengths. If you don't have the perfect-sized zipper, you can shorten long zippers with small nylon coils (but not metal or heavy-duty ones). Shorten a zipper by stitching across the bottom a few times using a zigzag stitch. This creates a faux stopper for the zipper. After you have completed the new zipper stop, cut off the excess zipper.

Regular zippers are also important to know about, and because we are all about styling our projects, remember that they can be fun to use as a decoration.

Zippers can be tricky, and you will need to practice inserting them. Let's get some practice now and make a simple zipper pouch to get us started. You can use the pouch to keep your small sewing supplies (needles, pins, thread, buttons) together.

project:
Simple Zipper Pouch

WHAT YOU NEED

★ ¼ yard of a light- to medium-weight cotton fabric

★ 7″ invisible zipper

★ Basic sewing supplies

★ Iron

★ Zipper foot for your sewing machine

LET'S MAKE IT

1 Cut 2 rectangles 8″ × 9″ from the fabric.

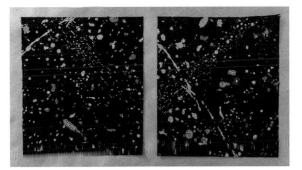

2 Open up the zipper and iron the teeth (the nylon coils) as flat as you can. Use a cool iron and keep the zipper open. Ask an adult to help since you are using the iron.

3 Lay the rectangles out, right sides up, with the top 8″ edges facing (where the zipper goes).

4 Place an outside edge of the zipper tape on the opening side of a fabric rectangle. Put it about ¼″ in from the edge, and right side down (so the zipper pull is facing down, and you see the flat back side up). Pin in place.

5 Put the zipper foot on your sewing machine, then put the pinned zipper and fabric piece under the zipper foot as shown. The zipper foot should line up as close as possible with the teeth, but not on top. Sew along the zipper as close to the zipper pull as you can.

6 Match the other side of the zipper to the right side of the other fabric rectangle like in Step 4, pin, and sew like in Step 5.

7 Hand sew the zipper to the rectangles from where you stopped sewing on the machine.

8 Close the zipper halfway, match the right sides of the 2 fabric rectangles, and pin and sew around the 3 open sides. Press your seams open.

9 Clip the corners and turn your pouch right side out.

Fashion Designing

FASHION ILLUSTRATION

Another great way to discover your *creative style* is to do some fashion illustration. Whether you have an entire collection in mind, an outfit you want to make, or just one piece, fashion illustration gives you (and others) a visual representation of what your specific vision is.

Most fashion designers are constantly drawing their designs for their collections. They work from these drawings to consider various fabrics and ultimately to choose fabrics and make the garment.

Some designers draw their designs freehand. Some use croquis.

A croquis is a sketched drawing of a human figure that is used in fashion design.

It provides a well-proportioned fashion figure for you to draw your garments and accessories on. You have your own croquis to color and design on (page 45)! Trace a croquis using lightweight paper or vellum (what the fashion designers use) or make photocopies of the page so you have lots of croquis on hand to use and design.

Patterns (page 44) of different pieces of clothing and boots are also blank and will help you draw the various fashion silhouettes. Trace over them again and again if you use lightweight paper for your croquis, copy them with a photocopier, or make templates (page 33) on a heavier paper or cardboard so you can use them over and over.

Experiment with modifying the patterns as you trace them. For example, don't trace the arms on the shirt and you have a tank top! Or trace only the top part of the pants and you have shorts. Use your observation skills as well as your imagination and creativity.

Use markers or colored pencils. Take some fabric swatches and paste them on the side of the page for more inspiration. Add some sparkle if you like by drawing in some jeweled accessories, and maybe even sticking samples of what you like next to the design as well.

Don't forget to draw hair and a face on your croquis. Your design should be personal and have a personality!

Texture!

Create unique textures by using some household items. Trace over sandpaper to give your garment the look of denim. Dot some correction fluid on the designs and color over them to create the look of sequins. Look around your house for textures and do rubbings to create different looks. But it might be challenging to find a fabric that duplicates the look. You'll have to use your imagination!

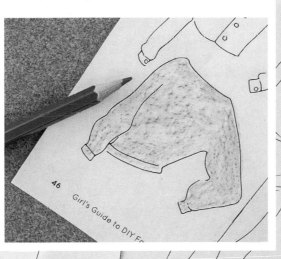

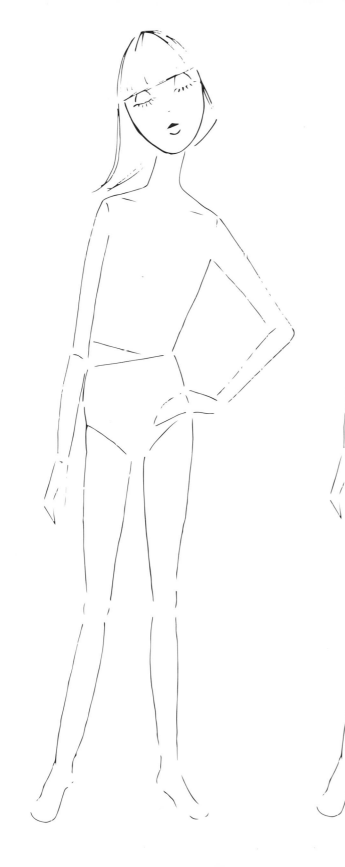

Practice some basic fashion illustration.

Back to School

The outfit for the first day seems to always be top of mind. Now that you are learning to sew and craft, you can make your outfit like no one else's and really stand out. Sound fun?

Let's make this outfit a reflection of you and your style. Maybe you are inspired by one of the mood boards or fashion illustrations you made. In this section the outfit is all about a playful and chic skirt paired with a cardigan (a sweater that opens in the front) and fun accessories you can make and style.

Let's do a little designing before we get started.

Here is a sketch of the outfit we will make. Grab some markers or colored pencils, and maybe some fabric swatches too, and color, doodle, and show how you would like your outfit to look. Then we can get to stitching. On the following pages I show you the steps to make it!

Double Layer Skirt

WHAT YOU NEED

- ★ ½ to ¾ yard each of 2 different fabrics*
- ★ Knit non-roll elastic, 1˝ wide
- ★ Basic sewing supplies
- ★ Pattern or kraft paper
- ★ Flat ruler
- ★ Pencil
- ★ Plain paper

*Use a light- to medium-weight cotton. Denim or corduroy is also an option.

LET'S PREP

(1) Use your measurements (page 27) to figure out how much fabric and elastic you need. Fill in the blanks below to determine the correct dimensions you will use to draw your pattern.

Waist: _____

Hips: _____

Distance from waist to knee: _____

1. [____] + 8″ = [____] **(A)**   This is how big around your skirt will be.

　Hip
　measurement

2. [____] ÷ 2 = [____] **(B)**   This is how wide your pattern piece will be.

　A

3. [____] + 2½″ = [____] **(C)**   This is how long the bottom layer of your skirt will be.

　Waist-to-knee
　measurement

4. [____] − 6″ = [____] **(D)**   This is how long the top layer of your skirt will be.

　C

5. [____] − 1″ or 2″ = [____] **(E)**   This is the length to cut the elastic. Don't stretch it when cutting.

　Waist

Woot, woot! Math!
That's right. People who sew are smart and stylish!

(2) You are making a pattern piece that is only half as wide as the number for A.

Divide A by 2 to get B. Draw a rectangle with that number as the width and C as the length for the bottom layer. Mark the width and the length on the pattern and label it *Bottom Layer*.

Example

(A) *If my hips are 33″ + 8″ = 41″*

(B) *41″ ÷ 2 = 20½″*
My pattern piece should measure 20½″ across.

(C) *If the distance from my waist (the part of your waist where you would like the skirt to sit) to my knee (where I want the bottom of the skirt to hit) is 16″ + 2½″ = 18½″*

(D) *My pattern piece should measure 18½″ up and down.*

A÷2
20½″
B+2½″   18½″
Bottom Layer

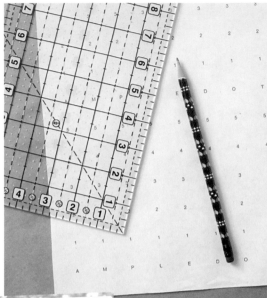

GOT ENOUGH FABRIC?

Most of the time you will cut this skirt across the width of your fabric. That means you need to buy a little more yardage than the numbers for C and D.

If measurement A is bigger than the width of the fabric you would like to use, buy as much fabric as measurement A. (Fabric for clothes is usually 40″–45″ wide or 60″ wide.) For example, if you need 50″ for A, and you want to use 45″-wide fabric, then buy 1⅓ yards of fabric. Keep the extra fabric. It could come in handy for some of the other projects in the book!

③ Draw a rectangle the same width as in Step 2 and the length of D for the top layer. Mark the width and the length on the pattern and label it *Top Layer*.

Example

B *My top layer is the same width*

D *The height of my rectangle is 18½″ – 6″ = 12½″*

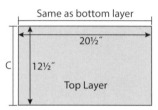

④ Cut your paper patterns out.

⑤ Cut 1 piece of elastic the length you wrote down for E.

Example

E *If my waist is 24″ then I would cut a piece of elastic that measures 23″.*

6 Fold the bottom-layer fabric right sides together, lining up the selvage edges, so you have a double layer. Pin your pattern to the fabric, with the length lined up on the fold of the fabric. This way, you will cut a piece that is twice as wide as the width of the pattern. (That's why you divided A in half back in Step 2.) Place the pins so they line up with the edge of the pattern (see Pinning, page 34).

7 Repeat Step 6 with your second fabric for the top layer.

8 Trace around the patterns carefully with your fabric marker. Remove the pattern pieces and save them in a safe place.

9 Cut both pieces out along the traced lines.

WHICH WAY DOES IT GO?

If you are using a printed fabric that has a direction, check to make sure that it will be facing in the right direction when the skirt is sewn. Sometimes it's helpful to write *Top* on your pattern pieces so they get cut correctly. Pay attention when pinning, too.

Sometimes you need to put the pattern piece in a different direction (like sideways) so the print will look right when it is cut and sewn. If the fabric isn't wide enough, you could cut two pieces and sew them together. Think about this before you buy your fabric, because it may change how much fabric you need.

LET'S CREATE!

Sew with a ⅝″ seam allowance unless the instructions say otherwise.
Backstitch at the beginning and end of all seams. Press the seam allowances
open after each seam.

(1) Unfold the skirt pieces. With right sides together, pin and sew the 2 short sides of the bottom-layer piece together. Follow the same steps for the top layer.

FINISHING SEAM ALLOWANCES

You can finish the seam allowances (to keep them from fraying) by trimming them with pinking shears after you sew the seams but before you press them open. You can also zigzag stitch along each individual seam allowance or serge them if you know how to use a serger.

(2) Hem the bottom edge of the top layer only, following the directions in How to Hem (page 35). You are hemming the top layer earlier than usual because it is easier to do before attaching the 2 layers.

(3) Put the top layer inside the bottom layer. The wrong sides of both fabrics should be facing out. Line them up at the side seams and all around the top edge. It should look like a giant tube.

(4) Pin together all around at the top. Mark a line 1½″ down from the top all around, or set your sewing machine to sew with a 1½″ seam allowance. Sew the layers together as marked. This will keep the layers together when you make the casing for the elastic.

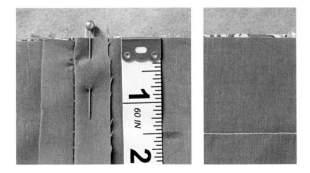

5 Follow Creating a Casing, Step 1 (page 36), to fold, press, and pin the top edge over to the wrong side on the stitching line.

6 Follow Creating a Casing, Steps 2–5 (page 36), to mark the opening, sew the casing, and feed the elastic through the casing.

LET'S FINISH

This is a good time to try the skirt on to make sure it fits.

1 Unpin the elastic, overlap the ends 1″, and pin them together with a safety pin. Try the skirt on. If the waist is too loose, make it tighter by overlapping the elastic more; if it is too tight, overlap the ends a little less.

2 Follow Creating a Casing, Steps 6 and 7 (page 37), to sew the elastic together and sew the casing the rest of the way closed.

3 Try the skirt on again and mark or pin how short you would like the bottom layer to be. See How to Hem (page 35) for steps to hem the bottom layer.

EMBELLISH!

Jazz your skirt up by adding some colorful ribbon or pom-poms to the bottom tier!

Easy Skirt Alternative

For a simpler version of this project, you can opt to do one layer. You can really showcase a super-cute fabric. Just follow the steps for the bottom layer.

Flirty Floral Cardigan

WHAT YOU NEED

★ Solid-colored cardigan sweater (one you have in your closet or a new one)

★ ¼ yard of fabric or scraps (all the same or a few different fabrics)

★ Felt (either scraps or 1 sheet 9″ × 12″)

★ Buttons or beads for the flower centers

★ Hand-sewing needle

★ Basic sewing supplies

★ Cardboard or heavy paper

LET'S PREP

We are trimming the collar with flowers made of fabric and felt.

(1) Trace the circle pattern (on pullout page P4) onto cardboard or heavier paper. Cut it out. This will be your template.

(2) Measure the front of the neckline, from shoulder to shoulder as shown. If you want to add flowers all the way around, then measure all the way around the front and back. A tape measure will be easier to use than a flat ruler.

(3) Determine how many flowers will fit around the neckline. You can just use the cardboard template or do the math. Each flower is 1½˝ wide. Divide the neckline measurement by 1½˝ to see how many flowers will fit. Round down to a whole number.

Example

If the measurement is 10˝:

10˝ ÷ 1.5˝ = 6.7

We will make 6 flowers (not 7, because you don't want them squished together).

(4) Trace and cut out as many circles from felt as you figured in Step 3. Put those aside; they will anchor your flowers.

(5) Multiply the number of flowers from Step 3 by 6. Trace and cut out this many circles out of your fabric(s) using the circle template.

THINGS TO REMEMBER

★ *Make sure that your sweater is washed and clean.*

★ *You can also replace the buttons. Remove them with small scissors or a seam ripper before getting started. Use buttons the same size as the original ones. See Buttons (page 37) for sewing tips.*

LET'S CREATE!

(1) Let's make the flowers. Thread the hand-sewing needle with coordinating thread and knot it at the end. Stick the needle through the bottom of the felt circle until the thread is stopped by the knot.

(2) Fold 1 fabric circle in half and then in half again.

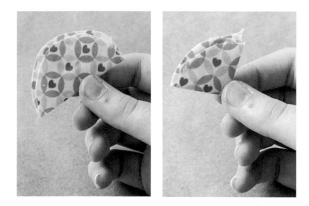

(3) Hold the folded fabric circle in place on top of the felt circle. Lining up the edges, make 2 or 3 stitches through the layers at the point. Make sure the fabric is secure.

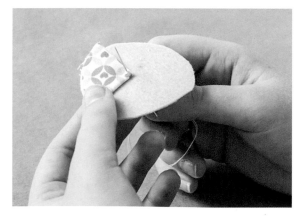

(4) Repeat Steps 1–3 to go all around the felt circle with the first 4 fabric circles. Then layer and stitch the last 2 on top.

(5) With your threaded needle, stitch a button in the center. You can also use a pretty bead. Stitch a few times on the back to secure it in place (this is even stronger than a knot).

6 Pin your flowers around the neckline of the sweater.

7 Push the fabric flower "petals" out of the way and stitch around the felt circle with your sewing machine to attach each flower to the sweater. You can also hand sew them using a running stitch (page 16). The fabric petals will hide your stitches.

Style It!

★ Create your own design: Draw a pattern of what you would like to stitch onto your sweater—think hearts, stars, a funky shape, you name it! Think about scale and what will look best on your sweater. Make a template and follow Steps 6 and 7 (at left) to attach your creation to your sweater.

★ Are you a pocket girl? Add pockets to the front of the cardigan. Decide how big you want your pockets and add 1˝ to this number. Cut out 2 squares of your leftover fabric or felt. Hem (page 35) the top edge ½˝. Fold and press the remaining 3 sides ½˝ to the wrong side. Pin and topstitch (see Sewing Words, page 33) the pockets to the cardigan by machine. Or hand sew using a whipstitch (see Basic Hand Sewing, page 16).

★ Use your designs as elbow patches! I suggest hand sewing these in place because it might get tricky to sew them in place with the machine. Use a whip-stitch (see Basic Hand Sewing, page 16).

Pretty Pencil Case

WHAT YOU NEED

- ★ ¼ yard of fabric for the outside
- ★ ¼ yard of fabric for the lining
- ★ Invisible zipper, 9˝ long

- ★ Wool felt, 2 or 3 colorful sheets (usually available 12˝ × 18˝ or smaller)
- ★ Fusible web

- ★ Basic sewing supplies
- ★ Flat ruler
- ★ Zipper foot
- ★ Pencil
- ★ Plain paper

I like to use an invisible zipper, but there are also some bold and bright regular zippers with colorful teeth available.

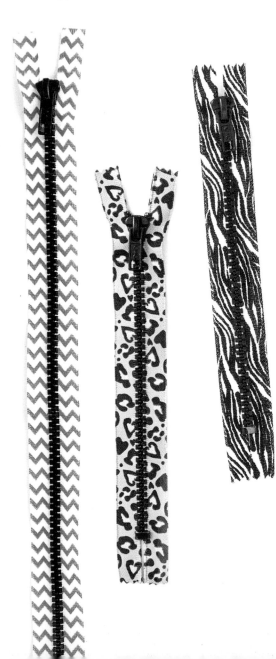

LET'S PREP

1 Use a flat ruler, pencil, and paper to draw a rectangle 9″ × 10″. Cut it out and label it *Pouch Pattern*. The 9″ edges will be the top and bottom.

2 Fold each fabric in half, right sides together. Pin and trace the pouch pattern on the double layer of each fabric. Cut the pieces out. You should have 4 rectangles. Use an erasable fabric marker or a pin to mark the top 9″ edge of each piece.

Fusible Appliqué

1 Trace the appliqué shapes (choose what you like from pullout page P4) onto the paper side of the fusible web. Cut them out roughly.

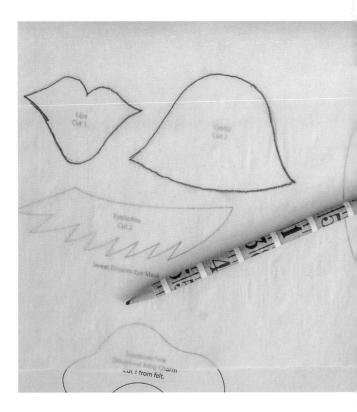

2 Following the instructions that came with the fusible, iron the shapes to your felt. Make sure the piece of felt is bigger all around, or you'll get sticky gunk on your iron or ironing board. Trim the extra fusible web if you need to. Be careful of the hot iron, too.

3 When the fusible is cooled off, cut out all the shapes right on the traced lines. Be careful when cutting those curvy lines; go slow.

Caution! Hot!

LET'S CREATE!

Sew with a ¼" seam allowance unless the instructions say otherwise. Backstitch at the beginning and end of all seams. Press the seam allowances open after each seam.

1 Peel the paper off the back of each appliqué. Lay an outside fabric piece right side up. Pin your appliqués, fusible side down, where you would like them.

2 Iron the appliqués in place.

(3) Stitch around the edges of the appliqués by machine or hand to double secure them.

(4) See the Simple Zipper Pouch (page 38) for practice if you have not sewn an invisible zipper before. Lay 1 outside fabric piece right side up. Open up your zipper and put it face-down on the top edge of the fabric as shown. (The zipper pull should be facing down.) Pin the top edge of the zipper tape in place ¼″ down from the top edge of the fabric.

(5) Lay 1 piece of lining fabric on top of the zipper/outside fabric piece, right sides together. Line them up at the top and pin them together. The zipper should be sandwiched between the 2 fabrics.

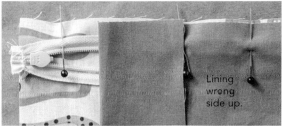

Lining wrong side up.

(6) Put the zipper foot on your machine. Follow the instructions in Simple Zipper Pouch, Step 5 (page 39), to sew through all 3 layers.

(7) Repeat Steps 4–6 to pin and sew the other outside and lining pieces to the other side of the zipper tape in the exact same way.

(8) Lay the pieces out flat with the zipper in the center. Make sure to leave the zipper unzipped for now. Match up the outside pieces, right sides together, and pin around the open edges. Do the same thing with the lining pieces, but mark a 2″–3″ gap on the bottom edge of the lining to leave open for turning the pouch right side out.

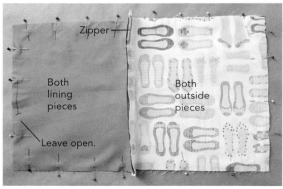

Zipper

Both lining pieces

Both outside pieces

Leave open.

LET'S FINISH

(1) Sew all around the open pouch you just pinned—except for where you marked. Start at an end of the mark, pivot at each corner, and end at the other end of the mark.

(2) Cut off the square corners at an angle. This makes them flatter. Be careful not to cut your stitching.

(3) Press the seams open.

(4) Turn the pouch right side out. Push the seam allowances on the opening in the lining inside and sew it closed by hand or machine. Then stuff the lining into the outside.

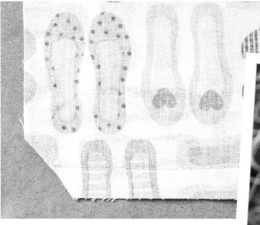

The best part about making something for myself is being able to use and/or wear what I sew.

Hannah, 15

Totally Tights

WHAT YOU NEED

★ Plain, solid-colored tights (Stay away from textured ones.)

★ Fabric paint (or acrylic paint)

★ Small sponge, paintbrush, or roller

★ About ⅓ of a small roll of contact paper (Make sure it is the kind that has a sticky back—stores call that "self-adhesive.")

★ Paper punch of a small design, such as a heart, star, or circle

★ Medium- to heavyweight paper big enough to cut into strips the length of your tights (Try waxed paper or freezer paper.)

LET'S PREP

(1) Use the paper punch to make a bunch (about 200) of the design from the contact paper. Space the designs about 1½″ apart. You don't need the punched-out pieces, so you can throw them away or find another use for them.

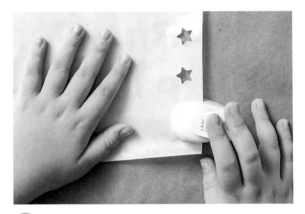

(2) Cut apart all the punched-out shapes so you have lots of pieces with 1 design punched in the center. Don't cut too close to the hole— leave at least ¼″. These are your stencils.

(3) Measure the width and length of a leg of your tights. Cut 2 strips of the medium- to heavyweight paper to those dimensions. Slip 1 strip in each leg. This will prevent the paint from bleeding to the other side.

LET'S CREATE!

(1) Lay out your tights on a flat surface and tape them down. Peel off the back of the contact paper and stick the stencils randomly on the tights. (Save half the stencils for the other side!) Make sure the contact paper is pressed down well so paint will not bleed underneath.

(2) Dab paint over each stencil you stuck onto the tights. Do your best not to paint beyond the outside edge of the contact paper. Apply a second coat if you want more color.

KEEP IT NEAT

Make sure to lay down some newspaper or kraft paper so you don't get paint on anything you—or the adults around you—don't want painted!

(3) Let your tights dry, anywhere from 4 to 8 hours.

(4) Remove the contact paper stencils. Untape and flip the tights over.

(5) Repeat Steps 1–3 on the other side. Use the stencils you saved earlier.

LET'S FINISH

When it's dry, peel off the cutouts, and it's done.

Stamp It!

Instead of using punches, find a stamp of a design you like. With a stamp, you skip the contact paper, punching, and cutting anything out. Just dip your stamp in paint and, well, stamp. You still want to slip paper inside the tight legs, and the tights will still need drying time on each side. Wash your stamps when you are done.

Style It!

★ You might want big designs freehand painted on your tights. It's your design; go for it!

★ You might want to just paint a design on the knees. I love the idea of big hearts or smiley faces. Try the tights on beforehand and mark where the knees are so you know where to paint.

Fun with Friends

I bet that for many of you, one of your favorite things to do is spend time with your friends. I bet it doesn't matter whether it's during school, after school, or on weekends. Anytime is a good time with your BFF or bestie! Am I right?

Now, what to wear for this good time? Why not design and make an outfit yourself? Now that you are learning to sew and design, you can really create whatever style you like. And when your friends say, "I LOVE that!" and ask, "Where did you get it?" you can proudly say, "I made it!" You could even invite your friends to sew with you. How great is it to come up with ideas together and share them?

In this section, you will make and style a few basic clothing items and accessories. Show off your creative style; it will surely be *Fun with Friends*.

Let's do a little designing before we get started.
Use the uncolored sketch of the outfit we will make. Grab some markers or colored pencils, or even some fabric swatches, and show how you would like your outfit to look. Then we can get to stitching!

Jeggings

WHAT YOU NEED

* ★ 1–1½ yards of knit fabric (Check your size, page 27, to figure out how much fabric to buy, page 69.)

* ★ Knit non-roll elastic, 1″ wide (See Let's Prep, Step 4, page 70, to figure out how much you need.)

* ★ Basic sewing supplies

* ★ Pattern paper

* ★ Pencil

We made the jeggings in the photo longer. The pattern is a cropped style (depending on your height) but you can easily change the length (page 29).

We will be using a knit fabric. Review the section Stitching with Knit (page 19). Choose a knit fabric that is made of 5% or more Lycra. This way the jeggings (or leggings) will mold and fit to your body—you do not want saggy pants!

How Much Fabric to Buy

Fabric width	Size 7	Size 8	Size 10	Size 12	Size 14
44″/60″	1 yard	1¼ yards	1¼ yards	1¼ yards	1¼ yards

My favorite thing to sew is leggings and skirts.

Samantha, 11

LET'S PREP

See How to Use Patterns (page 28) for tips.

(1) Trace the jeggings pattern (on pullout page P3) in the correct size onto your pattern paper. Copy any markings from the original onto your pattern piece. Cut out 1 paper pattern.

Hold the pattern piece up to yourself to check the length.

If you want your pants longer, now is the time to make the pattern longer (page 29).

If you want your pants a lot shorter (page 29), it's easier to do that now too!

(2) Fold your fabric right sides together, matching up the selvages. Pin the jeggings pattern on top. Make sure the grainline is parallel (in line with) the selvages.

Anatomy of Pants

The rise: The distance from the middle of the crotch seam that is right between your legs to the top of your waistband.

The inseam: The inside seam of a pant leg that goes all the way from one ankle up to the crotch (so a pair of pants has 2 inseams that are the same length).

The outseam: The seam on the outside of your pants from the waistband down to the hem.

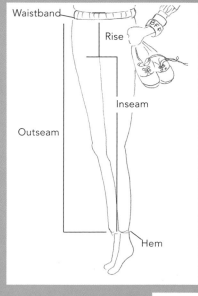

Waistband · Rise · Inseam · Outseam · Hem

3 Trace the pattern onto the fabric. Cut it out through both layers. You will have 2 pieces. Mark "front rise" and "back rise" and the notches from the pattern onto the fabric with your fabric-marking tool.

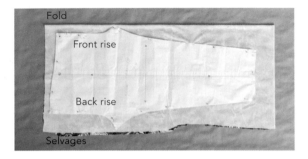

4 Measure around your waist. Cut 1 piece of elastic 1–2″ shorter.

LET'S CREATE!

See Stitching with Knit (page 19) to adjust your stitch settings and choose the correct needle for your fabric. Sew with a ⅝″ seam allowance unless the instructions say otherwise. Backstitch at the beginning and end of all seams. When sewing knits, you don't need to press your seam allowances.

1 With right sides together, pin along the 2 top curves on each side, marked *Front rise* and *Back rise* on the pattern. Match up the notches. Notice that the back rise is a bit bigger.

DON'T MOVE!

Sometimes knit or spandex fabric can get slippery. Taping the fabric down to your working surface helps keep it from moving. You want it to stay flat and smooth, but don't stretch it out.

I loved sewing leggings. I got to pick the coolest fabric and finally have leggings that are long enough for me! I get tons of compliments when I wear them and it makes me feel proud that I made them from scratch. — Bobbi, 11

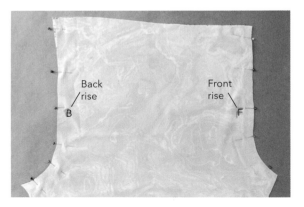

(2) Sew the 2 curved rise seams you just pinned. You will have a tube at the top with 2 open legs hanging down loose.

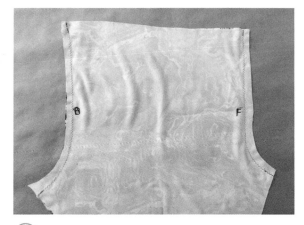

(3) Pull the legs apart and match up the rise seams in the center. The 2 legs should be hanging down loose. Fold 1 leg right sides together and match up the inseam and notches. Pin the leg together from the ankle up to the rise seam. Open up the seam allowances of the rise seams and pin them flat. Repeat with the other leg.

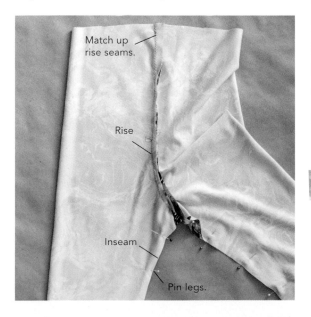

(4) Sew the inseams from an ankle up to the rise seam (crotch) and back down to the other ankle without stopping. Go slowly along the curved crotch.

(5) See Creating a Casing (page 36) to sew the waistband casing, insert the elastic, and then sew the elastic and casing closed. Keep using the zigzag stitch for these steps, since you're using a knit fabric.

LET'S FINISH

(1) Try on your jeggings to see if you want them any shorter. If you do, mark where you want the pants to end with a fabric marker or pins.

(2) If there is a lot of extra fabric at the bottom, mark a line 1½˝ below your mark. Cut off the extra length.

(3) Hem using the zigzag stitch. (See How to Hem, page 35.)

TIP Mark the inside of your jeggings so you'll know the front from the back. Write *back* or your name or put a fun symbol using a fabric marker, Sharpie, or stamp. You know which side is the back because you marked the back rise in the beginning and the back is slightly higher.

Amazing Appliqué Sweatshirt

WHAT YOU NEED

★ Solid-colored sweatshirt (preferably a flat-front crewneck)

★ Fabric scraps, 1 per each design, and as big as the design you want to use (Neon or sparkly spandex fabrics are fun.)

★ Pom-pom or large button (*optional*)

★ Fusible web, like Heat*n*Bond

★ Basic sewing supplies

LET'S PREP

Read through the Let's Prep and Let's Create! sections for the Pretty Pencil Case (page 58) for step-by-step photo instructions for fusible appliqué.

(1) Choose 1 or more appliqué patterns (on pullout page P4) for the design on your sweatshirt.

(2) Trace each pattern onto the paper side of the fusible web.

(3) Cut the appliqué shapes out of the fusible roughly outside the traced line.

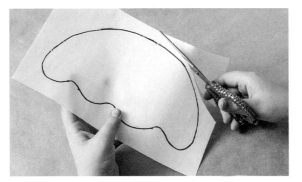

LET'S CREATE!

Read and follow the instructions that came with your fusible web before starting this project. Backstitch at the beginning and end of all stitching.

(1) Iron the fusible shapes to the wrong side of the appliqué fabric(s). Make sure the piece of fabric is bigger all around, or you'll get sticky gunk on your iron or ironing board. Trim the fusible web if needed. Be careful of the hot iron, too.

Make Your Own

This is your opportunity to get really creative and either use the designs included or draw your own. Keep the design simple so that it can be cut out of fabric. Use some plain white paper and a pencil. How about the first letter of your name, a favorite word or saying, or the face of an animal? Keep in mind the scale—how large you want your appliqué. And if your design has a left and a right side, like the letter R, you'll need to flip it over and trace it again so your design doesn't end up reversed when it's finished. You could also draw smaller designs and put them all over the sweatshirt, even on the back—the fun is really adding your own style to it. Make sure to collect enough fabric, as the exact amount depends on what the design will be, so it may vary.

 TIP If you aren't using plain cotton fabric, test fusing scraps of your appliqué fabric onto a bigger scrap so you get the iron settings right. I usually use a hot, dry iron with Heat*n*Bond Ultrahold and it works really well.

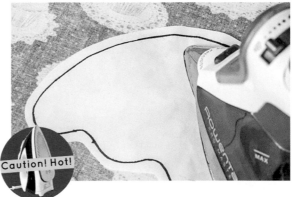

Caution! Hot!

2) When the fusible is cooled off, cut out all the shapes right on the traced lines. Peel the paper off the back of each appliqué.

3) Lay your sweatshirt out flat and smooth out any wrinkles. Pin the appliqués in place, right side up, so you can hold it up to yourself and look in the mirror to make sure it is where you would like it. Be careful of the pins!

4) Iron the center of the design lightly to the sweatshirt. Remove the pins and iron the entire design until it is completely stuck to the sweatshirt.

LET'S FINISH

Read the directions that came with the fusible web to see how you will need to wash and dry the sweatshirt to keep the appliqué looking good.

Hand sew a pom-pom or button on top of the cupcake, if you like.

STRONGER FINISH

Depending on the type of fusible web you used, you might need to sew it in place to permanently secure it. This can get tricky, so go slowly. Hand sewing is also an option. Try using a bold and colorful thread so the stitches stand out. Sew along the edge of the design using a zigzag stitch.

Style It!

Take this project one step further ...

★ This looks great with a loose-fitting or oversized sweatshirt.

★ Choose a new length for your sleeves, and cut the sleeves off an inch longer than you want. Roll up the raw edges and sew in place with a fun-colored thread.

★ Add another design.

★ Add a pocket (page 86) and hand sew on chain or ribbon to look like the strap of a cross-body purse.

★ Cut any ribbing or the hem off at the bottom of the sweatshirt and replace it with a strip of fun fabric or a trim.

Nifty Necklace

WHAT YOU NEED

★ 3 yards of pom-pom trim (if you want to mix 2 kinds or colors, approximately 2 yards of each)

★ 2 small key rings

★ ¾–1 yard of grosgrain ribbon

★ Basic sewing supplies

★ Hot glue gun

LET'S PREP

1 Measure around your neck 3 different lengths for your neck-lace. (You can make it just 1 or 2 strands if you prefer.)

2 Cut 1 piece of pom-pom trim for each measurement. There should be a short, a medium, and a long piece.

LET'S CREATE!

1 Lay the 3 strands out from shortest to longest. Pin the 3 ends together on both sides. Trim away any pom-poms that are in the way.

2 Sew the ends together, stitching back and forth using a zigzag stitch. If it's tricky to sew because it's small, use a glue gun instead.

(3) Fold about 1″ of an end of the triple strand around a key ring. Dab a bit of hot glue to secure it. Repeat with the other end and the other key ring.

LET'S FINISH

(1) Cut the ribbon in 2 equal pieces.

(2) Fold about 1″ of an end of ribbon around 1 key ring, opposite the trim. Hot glue it in place.

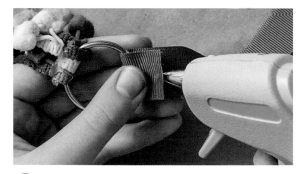

(3) Repeat Step 2 with the other key ring and other piece of ribbon.

(4) If you'd like, fold over the loose ends of the ribbon 2 times and topstitch for a nice finish.

(5) You're finished. Use the ribbon to tie the necklace around your neck. You can make the necklace shorter or longer depending on how you tie it, and if you tie a knot or a bow.

Make It with Beads

Another fun way to make a necklace is with fabric scraps, some beads, and a large-eye needle.

1. Cut a thin strip of fabric about ½″ wide and a few inches longer than you would like the necklace to hang around your neck.

2. Thread the scrap onto a large-eye needle and put the beads on.

Try using some fun letter beads and spell your favorite or most inspiring words. Or make a necklace for your best friend; spell out her name or just put *BFF*.

3. Tie a knot in the fabric on either side of the groups of beads.

4. Tie the ends together to wear the necklace.

Dynamite DIY Sneakers

WHAT YOU NEED

★ Plain canvas sneakers

★ Fabric paint or markers in 3–5 different colors

★ Pencil or erasable pen

★ Cardboard or heavy paper

★ Stiff, small-sized paint-brush (several if you are using multiple colors)

★ Cup of water

LET'S PREP

(1) Start with clean sneakers (they don't have to be new). Just wipe them down with a damp cloth and a little bit of soap and water or throw them in the washing machine and a not-too-hot dryer. Remove the laces.

(2) Trace the chevron pattern (on pullout page P4) onto cardboard or heavy paper and cut it out.

PROTECT IT

Because we are using paint or permanent markers for this project, I suggest covering the table or surface that you are working on. Newspaper or kraft paper is always good.

LET'S CREATE!

(1) Trace the chevron stripes onto your sneaker using a pencil or pen that's erasable, like the FriXion pens. You can do the tips or the entire sneaker. Just move the pattern over and match up the line if you

need to cover a longer area. Move the pattern up or down if you need to draw a second line to paint within. (You may not need a second line if you use wide-tipped paint markers. Just make stripes the width of the marker tip.)

(2) Using a stiff brush and fabric paint or fabric markers, color in the design. Try to stay within the lines. Change brushes when you change colors, and put the wet brush in a plastic bag so the paint won't dry out.

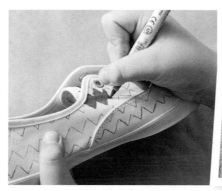

LET'S FINISH

(1) If you've used paint, let your sneakers dry overnight.

(2) Carefully put the laces back into the dry sneakers. Try them on.

Style It!

★ Swap the laces for fun, colorful laces or ribbon or actual lace.

★ String a few beads on the shoelaces for even more fun.

★ Use a freehand approach. Draw your own design in pencil and then color it in with fabric paint or markers. You can draw flowers or hearts or write your name— whatever feels right for your creative style.

Slumber Party

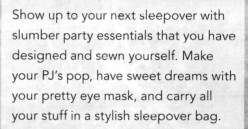

Show up to your next sleepover with slumber party essentials that you have designed and sewn yourself. Make your PJ's pop, have sweet dreams with your pretty eye mask, and carry all your stuff in a stylish sleepover bag.

Let's do a little designing before we get started.

Grab some markers or colored pencils, or even some fabric swatches, and use this uncolored sketch to show how you would like your outfit to look. Then we can get to stitching!

Peace Out Pajama Pants

WHAT YOU NEED

★ 1–2½ yards of cotton or flannel fabric (Check your size in How Much Fabric to Buy, page 83.)

★ Knit non-roll elastic, 1˝ wide (See Let's Prep, Step 4, page 83, to figure out how much you need.)

★ Basic sewing supplies

★ Safety pin

★ Iron

★ Pattern paper

We made the pajamas in the photo longer. You can easily change the length (page 29).

How Much Fabric to Buy

Fabric width		Size 7	Size 8	Size 10	Size 12	Size 14
	44″	1¾ yards	1¾ yards	2 yards	2 yards	2¼ yards
	60″	1 yard	1 yard	1¼ yards	1¼ yards	1¼ yards

LET'S PREP

See How to Use Patterns (page 28) for tips.

(1) Trace the pajama pant front and back patterns (on pullout pages P1 and P2) in the correct size onto your pattern paper. Copy any markings from the originals onto your 2 patterns. Cut out the paper patterns.

Hold the pattern pieces up to yourself to check the length.

If you want your pants longer, now is the time to make the patterns longer (page 29).

If you want your pants a lot shorter (page 29), it's easier to do that now too!

(2) Fold your fabric right sides together, matching up the selvages. Pin both pajama patterns on top. Make sure to line up the grainline marks with the selvages.

(3) Trace the patterns onto the fabric. Cut them out through both layers and mark the notches. You will have 4 pieces—2 fronts and 2 backs.

(4) Measure around your waist (or wherever you want your pants to sit). Cut 1 piece of elastic 1″–2″ shorter.

LET'S CREATE!

Sew with a ⅝″ seam allowance unless the instructions say otherwise. Backstitch at the beginning and end of all seams. Press the seam allowances open after each seam.

(1) Pin the 2 front pieces, right sides together, along the curved edge. This is the front rise (see Anatomy of Pants, page 69).

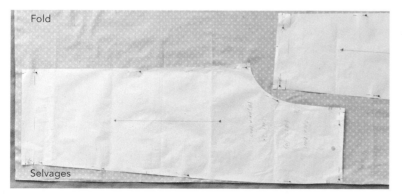

(2) Repeat Step 1 with the back pieces. This is the back rise.

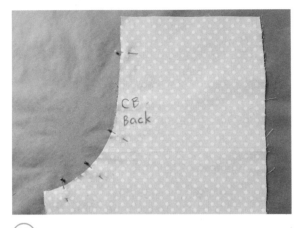

(3) Sew the front pieces together where you pinned. Repeat with the back pieces.

(4) Before you press the seam allowances open, snip little slits or triangles out of the curved area. Make sure not to cut into your stitches! This makes ironing easier. Then press the seam allowances open.

(5) Open up the sewn pieces. Match up the rise seams, right sides together, at the top and at the crotch. Then match up the front and back inseams (see Anatomy of Pants, page 69) of 1 leg, matching the notches, and pin together. Pin the other leg together the same way.

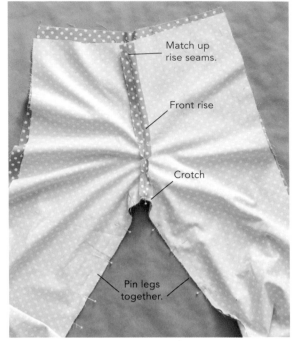

Match up rise seams.

Front rise

Crotch

Pin legs together.

(6) Sew the inseams from the bottom of a pant leg up to the crotch and back down the other pant leg without stopping.

(7) Pin the sides of a pant leg, right sides together. Sew the side seam. Repeat with the other pant leg.

(8) Refer to Creating a Casing (page 36) to make the waistband casing, thread the elastic, and sew up the elastic and the casing.

LET'S FINISH

Try on your pants. See How to Hem (page 35) to hem the pants as short as you like.

Waist

Side seam

Sleepover Tote

WHAT YOU NEED

★ ½ yard of fabric for the outside of the bag (If you choose a print fabric, look for one that looks good even if it's upside down.)

★ ½ yard of fabric for the inside of the bag

★ Flat gridded ruler

★ 1¼ yards of webbing for the straps, 1″–2″ wide

★ Basic sewing supplies

★ Pattern paper (optional)

LET'S PREP

(1) If you want, use the ruler to make a paper pattern that is a rectangle 16″ × 34″.

(2) Use your pattern or cut 1 rectangle that is 16″ × 34″ from each of your fabrics. Your bag will be folded at the bottom, so it will end up about half the length of the pieces you cut.

(3) Cut the webbing into 2 equal pieces.

LET'S CREATE!

Sew with a ½″ seam allowance unless the instructions say otherwise. Backstitch at the beginning and end of all seams. Press the seam allowances open after each seam.

(1) Fold both fabric pieces in half, matching up the 16″ ends, right sides together. The pieces should look almost square now. Press along the bottom folds to crease.

Add a Pocket

Add a pocket to your bag: use it to keep your good-luck charm, phone, mini music player, or anything you want to show your friends. Use any extra fabric or some scraps you have on hand. Make it as big or little as you like.

1. Use a flat ruler to draw a square or rectangle on fabric 1″ bigger than the pocket you want. Mine is 5½″ × 9″.

2. Cut it out.

3. Fold and press the top edge of the pocket over ½″ to the wrong side. Pin. Line up the edge of the presser foot with the fold, and sew.

4. Fold the other 3 sides over ½″ to the wrong side. Press.

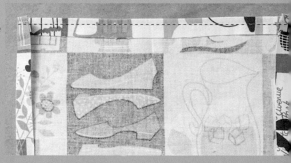

5. Put the pocket on top of the inside bag piece, both right side up. Pin it in place a few inches down from a short side as shown. Sew the pocket to the lining around just the sides and the bottom. Again, line the presser foot up with the edge of the folds when you sew.

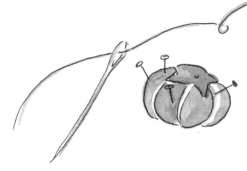

2 Add the pocket (page 86) now if you want it. Pin the long folded sides of the inside piece together. Pin the long sides of the outside piece together. Don't pin along the top edges.

3 Sew both pinned sides of the inside bag. Sew both pinned sides of the outside bag. Clip the corners off the seam allowances at the bottom.

4 Pull the sides of the inside bag apart and flatten it out. Line up a side seam with the bottom crease. It should look like a triangle. Just push the other bottom corner out of your way for now.

The best part of sewing is learning new and different things.

Samantha, 8

5 Use a flat ruler to measure 2″ from the point of the triangle along the side seam. Draw a line straight across, using your fabric-marking tool.

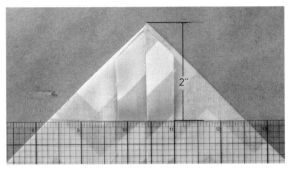

6 Sew on the line you just drew. This is called a boxed corner. It makes your bag wider so you can put more things in it.

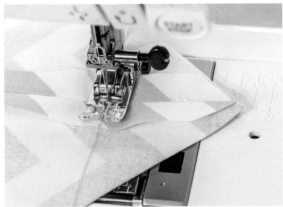

7 Now that you've done it once, repeat Steps 4–6 on the other corner of the inside bag and both corners of the outside bag.

8 Match up both bags at the bottom crease, wrong sides together. Pin an inside and an outside corner together on 1 end on the line. The side seams should be on the outside.

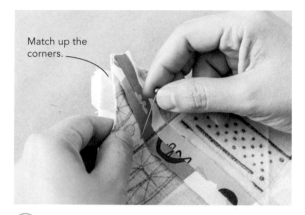

Match up the corners.

9 Sew the corners together on top of the line you just sewed. Cut the tips of the corners off about ½″ away from the seamline.

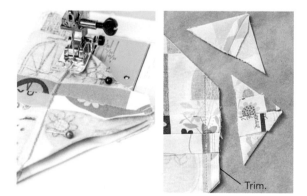

Trim.

10 Repeat Steps 8 and 9 to sew the 2 bags together at the other corner.

11 Pull the outside bag right side out over the lining, so the wrong sides are together.

Match up the side seams and put a pin in them at the top.

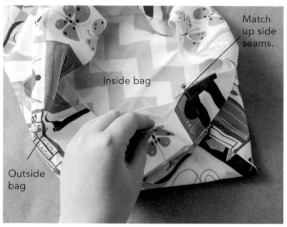

Match up side seams.

Inside bag

Outside bag

LET'S FINISH

1 Fold the top edges of the outside bag and the inside bag each ¾″ to the inside (wrong side). Iron all around to make a crease. Pin together all around the top.

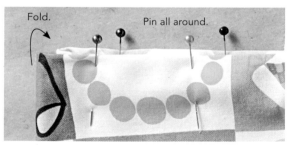

Fold.   Pin all around.

2 Mark 2″ (or wherever you would like your straps) in from each side seam at the top of the outside bag. Do this on both sides of the bag.

2″

(3) Pin an end of a piece of webbing between the top edges of the bag and the lining at a mark. Pin the other end of the webbing at the other mark on the same side. Make sure the webbing is not twisted. Pin the other piece of webbing to the other side of the bag in the same way.

Style It!

Add a cool design to your bag. Use any of the words or designs on pullout page P4 or draw your own. Use some fabric scraps and fusible web and follow the instructions for Amazing Appliqué Sweatshirt (page 72). It is best to attach the appliqués before you sew the outside bag together, but you can do it later, too.

(4) Topstitch all around the top of the bag. Start at a side seam. Line up the edge of the presser foot with the top of the bag. Sew over the ends of the webbing too, but be careful not to catch the straps!

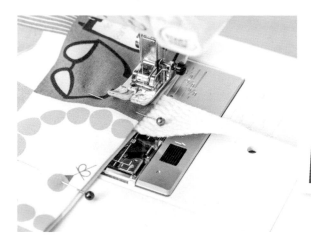

Stuffed Tote Charms

Add a stuffed charm to your tote! You can add one or as many as you want. Make them for your friends, too! How about a doughnut, a heart, or even lips? You can create your own design and use it as a pattern, or use one of the designs provided on pullout page P4.

WHAT YOU NEED

★ Assorted colored felt or fabric scraps

★ 2–3 colors of embroidery floss

★ Fiberfill for stuffing

★ 1 piece of rickrack 6˝ long for each charm

★ 1 key ring for each charm

★ Basic sewing supplies

★ Glue gun

Pick a pattern from the doughnut, heart, and lips on pullout page P4 or draw your own design. Follow the instructions in Tracing and Templates (page 29) to draw and cut out 2 of the same design from the fabric or felt scraps.

MAKE THE CHARMS

For the doughnut

1. Glue the icing onto the doughnut top.

Caution! Hot!

2 Use different colors of embroidery floss and a straight stitch to stitch some sprinkles on the icing.

3 Whipstitch (page 16) the doughnut top and bottom, wrong sides together all around the inner circle. Then stitch around the outside, leaving a 2″ opening so you can stuff the doughnut later. This is how you want to put together any shape with an opening in the middle, like the letter O.

For the lips

1 Pin the 2 lip pieces *right sides together*.

2 Sew around the edges with a ¼″ seam allowance. Use the edge of the presser foot as a guide. Leave an opening at the top so you can stuff the lips later. You can also sew by hand.

3 Turn the lips right side out and push out the corners with a chopstick.

For the heart

1 Try trimming the top piece so it's a little smaller. This will give the heart an outlined look.

2 Pin the 2 heart pieces wrong sides together.

3 Machine or hand sew around the heart. Leave an opening at the top so you can stuff it later.

FINISH THE CHARMS

1 Stuff each charm with fiberfill.

2 Fold the rickrack in half to make a loop for each charm. Pin the cut ends of the loop inside the opening you left in the charm.

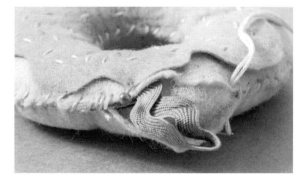

3 Sew the ends of the loop to the charm. Then sew the opening closed with a whipstitch (page 16).

4 Slide the key ring onto the loop.

Optional for the stuffed lips: If you like, draw a line across the middle of the stuffed lips. Sew on the line through the whole charm.

Sweet Dreams Eye Mask

WHAT YOU NEED

★ ¼ yard or a large scrap of cotton fabric

★ 1 sheet of colored felt or a large scrap of cotton batting

★ Different colored felt scraps for appliqués

★ Fusible web or fabric glue or hot glue gun

★ Basic sewing supplies

★ Coordinating thread

★ ½ yard of decorative elastic, ¼″–⅜″ wide.

★ Heavy paper or thin cardboard

★ Pencil

LET'S PREP

(1) Follow the instructions in Tracing and Templates (page 29) to make a template for the eye mask pattern (on pullout page P4). Copy the elastic placement marks too.

(2) If you want your mask to have fabric on both sides, pin, trace, and cut out 2 eye masks from fabric and 1 from the batting. If you want the back side to be felt, pin, trace, and cut out 1 eye mask from fabric and 1 eye mask from felt.

(3) Decide what appliqué designs on the pullout (page P4) you want on the front of your eye mask. The lowercase letters *d-r-e-a-m*, the eyelids and lashes, or the heart or regular sunglasses will all fit. Follow the instructions in Fusible Appliqué (page 59) to trace the patterns onto the fusible web, fuse them to the felt, and cut them out. (If you want, you can skip the fusible web and glue your cut-out appliqués on later.)

(4) Measure around the back of your head using a tape measure. Start right above your ear on one side and measure around to the top of the other ear. Add 1″ to this number. Cut 1 piece of elastic this length.

LET'S CREATE!

Sew with a ¼″ seam allowance unless the instructions say otherwise. Backstitch at the beginning and end of all seams. Press the seam allowances open after each seam.

1 Arrange your felt appliqués on the mask fabric, both right sides up. Follow the manufacturer's instructions to fuse the felt to the fabric. If you skipped the fusible step, glue the appliqués in place and wait for the glue to dry.

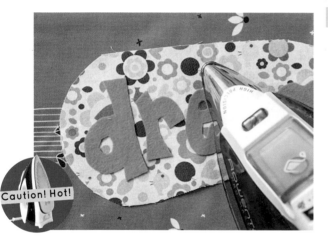

Caution! Hot!

2 Carefully stitch around the appliqués with your sewing machine or by hand using a running stitch (page 16).

3 Layer your pieces in this order:

back of mask, right side up if it's fabric (felt is the same on both sides)

elastic (as marked on the pattern)

front of mask, right side down

batting (if you are using it)

Pin the ends of the elastic at each side first. They should stick out about ½″ on each side. Then pin all around the mask.

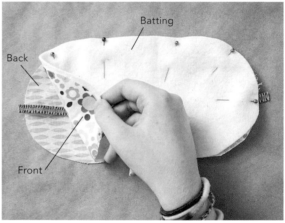

Batting

Back

Front

4 Along a straight edge of the mask, mark 1½″ to leave open for turning.

(5) Sew around the mask about ¼" from the edge. Line the edge of the mask up with the edge of the presser foot. Remember to stop where you marked the opening.

LET'S FINISH

(1) Snip into the curved part of the seam allowance a bit with small scissors. Make your cuts 1" or so apart. Don't cut through the stitches!

(2) Turn the mask right side out through the opening you left. Push out all the edges with a chopstick or the end of a pen or pencil. The cuts you made in the last step will help the seam allowances flatten out and the curves stay curved. Press the edges of the mask if you like.

(3) Topstitch around the edge of the mask. This will close up the opening too.

SEWING THE CURVE

You will be doing some curvy sewing for this step, so go SLOW. As you follow the curve you can always put your needle into the fabric using the balance wheel. Lift the presser foot, turn your fabric a bit to follow the curve, and then make sure to put the presser foot back down to start sewing again.

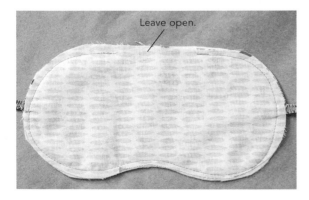

Leave open.

Rockin' Summer

Whether you spend your summers at sleepaway camp, on vacation, or home with your family, what you wear is important! In this section you will design and stitch up a ribbon tie dress and some fashionable flip-flops. Mix and match and make it your own. And feel free to add in favorite summer fashions that you already have in your closet.

Let's do a little designing before we get started.

Grab some markers or colored pencils, or even some fabric swatches, and use the uncolored sketch to show how you would like your outfit to look. Then we can get to stitching!

Ribbon Tie Dress

WHAT YOU NEED

★ ¾–1 yard of fabric at least 54˝ wide, such as lightweight cotton, voile, or knit (See Let's Prep, page 99, to figure out how much.)

★ 1½–2 yards of ribbon or rickrack, ½˝–1˝ wide (See Let's Prep, page 99, to figure out how much.)

★ Pattern paper

★ Basic sewing supplies

★ Safety pin

LET'S PREP

(1) Grab your measurements (page 27). You may need a friend and a measuring tape to take some new ones for this dress. Fill in the blanks below to get the correct dimensions you will use to make this dress a custom fit.

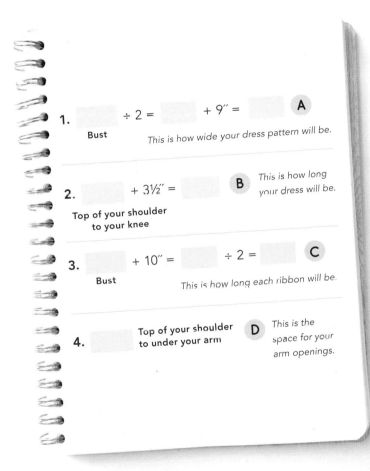

1. [____] ÷ 2 = [____] + 9″ = [____] **A**
   Bust   *This is how wide your dress pattern will be.*

2. [____] + 3½″ = [____] **B** *This is how long your dress will be.*
   Top of your shoulder to your knee

3. [____] + 10″ = [____] ÷ 2 = [____] **C**
   Bust   *This is how long each ribbon will be.*

4. [____] **Top of your shoulder to under your arm** **D** *This is the space for your arm openings.*

Éxample

A *My chest is 30″ ÷ 2 = 15″, then 15″ + 9″ = 24″.*

(2) Draw a rectangle that is as wide as A and as long as B on your pattern paper. Cut it out and label it *Ribbon Tie Dress*.

(3) You will need a little more fabric than B (the length of your dress) and twice as much ribbon as C.

CUTTING TIP

If you have lots of experience, skip making a pattern, and measure and mark out the rectangle right on your fabric.

(4) Fold your fabric right sides together, matching up the selvages. Pin your pattern piece in place. Trace it and cut it out through both layers. These 2 pieces are the dress front and dress back.

(5) Cut 2 pieces of ribbon to the length you wrote down for C. If you like, fold the ribbon ends over a bit to the wrong side and stitch across them. This will keep them from fraying. Or you can use Fray Check.

(6) On the wrong side of both the front and back pieces, mark the top of 1 short edge. Use a washable marker. Make the mark big enough for you to see it easily.

LET'S CREATE!

Sew with a ½″ seam allowance unless the instructions say otherwise. Backstitch at the beginning and end of all seams. Press the seam allowances open after each seam.

(1) Fold and press the long sides of the front and back pieces over ½″ to the wrong side. Pin down the entire length.

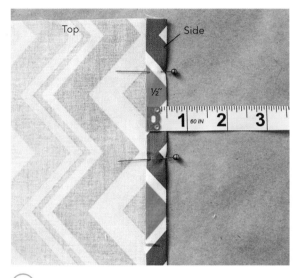

(2) Sew the pinned sides, lining up the edge of the presser foot with the fold.

(3) Fold and press the top edge of the front and back pieces over 1½″ to the wrong side. Pin along the edge.

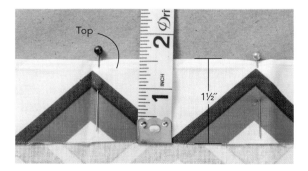

(4) Line up the left side of the presser foot with the cut edge of the front piece. Sew along the pinned section. This is the casing for the ribbon tie. Do the same for the back piece.

(5) Measure down from the top of 1 piece the amount you wrote for D. Mark this on the wrong side along both long sides. Match up the front and back, right sides together, at the top. Pin the long sides together from the mark all the way to the bottom.

6 Sew down 1 side from the mark all the way to the bottom of the dress. Repeat on the other side.

7 Grab a ribbon. Pin the safety pin to an end and use it to pull the ribbon through 1 casing. Stop when there's an even amount of ribbon on either end of the casing.

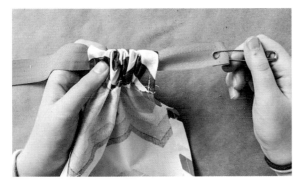

8 Bunch the casing up a bit, but not the ribbon. Safety-pin each end of the casing to hold the ribbon in place for now.

9 Repeat Steps 7 and 8 to feed the other ribbon through the other casing.

LET'S FINISH

1 Try the dress on. Tie the ribbons together over your shoulders. Undo the pins to add more or less bunching in the front and back if you like.

2 Once the length is just right, pin the ribbons in place at the ends of the casings. Sew across the ends of the casings to secure the ribbon.

3 Make sure your armholes are comfortable—not too short or too long—and adjust them if needed. You may need to stitch the side seams up a bit more to make the opening smaller or take some stitches out to make the openings longer. Don't forget to backstitch.

TIPS You can bunch the front and back more or less depending on how you want it to look. If you like more than one look, another option is to skip Step 2 above so you can change the look of the dress. Stitch a bit of the casing closed at the ends, but don't stitch through the ribbon. Always be careful that the ribbons do not come out.

It's up to you!

4 See How to Hem (page 35) to hem the dress as you like.

Make a Belt—It's a Cinch

1. Choose a fabric. Use the same fabric or choose a complementary color or print.

2. Cut a rectangle 5″ × 44″ from your fabric. (You can make your belt shorter by cutting a shorter rectangle. Or make it longer and you can wrap it around 2 or 3 times!)

3. Fold the rectangle in half, right sides together. Pin along the cut edges.

4. Sew along the long side where you pinned to make a long tube.

5. Put a safety pin in 1 end of the fabric tube. Push it through the tube to turn the belt right side out.

6. Fold the 2 short sides not sewn to the inside. Pin and topstitch close to each end.

Style It!

★ For a fun finishing touch, add a bit of trim or ribbon to the bottom of your dress. After you finish the hem, sew the trim along the bottom.

★ Use a wide ribbon as a belt.

★ Add pom-poms or fringe to the end of your belt. Or slip large beads on the belt and knot the ends.

Fabulous Flip-Flops

WHAT YOU NEED

- ★ Plain flip-flops
- ★ ⅛ yard of fabric
- ★ Assorted medium to large buttons or rhinestones
- ★ Glue gun

LET'S PREP

(1) Measure the length of the entire flip-flop strap (both sides). Add 6″–8″ to that number.

(2) Cut 4 strips of fabric the length you figured out in Step 1 and 1½″–2″ wide.

TIP If you don't want to see the cut edges of the fabric strips, cut the strips twice as wide. Fold each strip right sides together along the long edge. Sew along the long edges with a ¼″ seam allowance. Turn the fabric tube right side out and press it flat. Push the short ends in to the wrong side and topstitch the ends closed.

LET'S CREATE!

(1) Match up 2 strips, wrong sides together. Wrap the middle of the strips around the center of 1 flip-flop strap (the part that goes between your toes). Put a bit of hot glue there to keep them in place. You should have 2 loose ends on either side.

(2) Start on 1 side of the flip-flop strap. Separate the 2 fabric strips so there is 1 on either side of the strap. Braid the 2 fabric strips around the flip-flop strap—wrap 1 strip over and under the flip-flop strap, then the other. Repeat until the strap is covered. Make sure the right side of the fabric is facing up; it can get twisted. If you don't know how to braid, just wrap the fabric around the strap.

3 Glue the ends of the fabric strips to the end of the strap. Cut away any extra fabric. Grab an adult and use your glue gun.

Caution! Hot!

4 Repeat Steps 2 and 3 to braid around the other side of the flip-flop strap.

5 Repeat Steps 1–4 to cover the other flip-flop with fabric.

LET'S FINISH

Glue a medium- to large-sized button or rhinestone in the center of the straps at the top of each flip-flop as an added finishing touch.

Style It!

Get really creative and decorate your flip-flops with colorful buttons or rhinestones in a variety of sizes and cover each of the straps.

Hot Head Wrap

WHAT YOU NEED

★ ¼ yard of knit fabric (enough to make 2 to 3 head wraps)

★ Basic sewing supplies

LET'S PREP

(1) Measure around your head where you would wear a head wrap. If your knit fabric is really stretchy, subtract 2˝. If it's not so stretchy, subtract 1˝.

(2) Cut a rectangle from your fabric that is 6˝ wide by the number you figured out in Step 1.

(3) Cut a square of fabric about 3˝ × 3˝.

LET'S CREATE!

See Stitching with Knit (page 19) to adjust your stitch settings and choose the correct needle for your fabric. Sew with a ½˝ seam allowance unless the instructions say otherwise. Backstitch at the beginning and end of all seams. You don't need to press any seams for this project.

(1) Fold the larger piece of fabric in half lengthwise, right sides together, and pin.

(2) Sew along the long edge.

(3) You have created a tube; turn it right side out. Turn the raw edges of 1 end into the wrong side ½˝. Fold the tube in half and stick 1 end inside the folded-in end and pin them together.

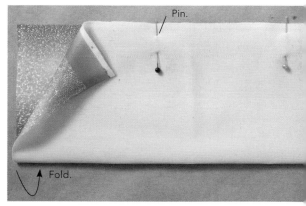

Pin.

Fold.

4 Hand sew the 2 ends together using a straight stitch.

5 Pull the thread to gather the fabric. Knot the thread and cut it off.

Try the head wrap on to see how it fits. If you need to make it bigger or smaller, rip out your stitches, adjust how much you overlap the ends, and sew them together again.

LET'S FINISH

1 Fold the smaller piece of fabric in half, right sides together. Pin and sew to make a tube. Turn it right side out.

2 Wrap the smaller tube around the gathered section of the head wrap. Line up the ends of the tube with the long seam. Pin it in place. This is the wrong side of the head wrap.

3 Fold the raw edges that are showing on top to the inside of the small tube. Hand sew the ends together using a whipstitch (page 16).

Style It!

Add a faux bow to the center of the head wrap.

1. Cut out a 3″ × 6″ rectangle of the same fabric as the head wrap.

2. Fold each of the 4 sides over ½″ to the wrong side and pin.

3. Sew all around close to the edges to hem the faux bow.

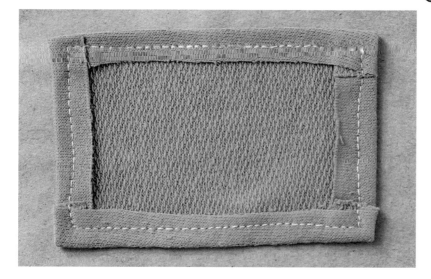

4. Slip the faux bow, right side up, inside the center loop on the head wrap. Sew it in place at the center with a few hand stitches.

Going to a Party

Do you love to go to a party? I know I do! Whenever I receive a party invitation, one of the first things I ask is: What am I going to wear? Then, to decide, I ask myself some other questions: What kind of party is it? Is there a theme? What time of year is it? With this information I get excited and start to envision all the possible looks I could put together. Lucky for us, we are all learning how to make our own clothes and accessories so we can design our own party outfit. How fun!

In this section you will make the essential party must-haves: a festive dress, a party purse, shoe clips, and the perfect party hair accessory—a glitter headband. Using your imagination you can style each piece to reflect your personality.

Let's do a little designing before we get started.

Here is a blank sketch of the outfit we will make. Grab some markers or colored pencils, and maybe some fabric swatches too, and color, doodle, and show how you would like your outfit to look. Then we can get to stitching!

Necklace Dress

WHAT YOU NEED

- ★ 1¼–2 yards of light- to medium-weight fabric (Check your size in How Much Fabric to Buy, page 113.)

- ★ Wool felt: sheets or scraps at least 9″ × 12″

- ★ ½ yard of ribbon, ¼″–⅝″ wide

- ★ Invisible zipper to match dress fabric, 15″ long

- ★ Rhinestones, different sizes and shapes: glue-on or sew-on

- ★ Glue gun or thread to match collar, depending on type of rhinestones

- ★ Basic sewing supplies

- ★ Pattern paper

- ★ Zipper foot

Fabric width		Size 7	Size 8	Size 10	Size 12	Size 14
	44″	1¼ yards	1¼ yards	1½ yards	1¾ yards	1¾ yards
	60″	1 yard	1 yard	1 yard	1¼ yards	1¼ yards

You may need more fabric if you use a print with a direction to it (see Which Way Does It Go?, page 51).

LET'S PREP

See How to Use Patterns (page 28) for tips.

(1) Trace the dress front and dress back patterns (on pullout pages P1 and P2) in the correct size onto your pattern paper. Copy any marks from the originals onto your pattern pieces. Cut out the paper patterns.

Hold the pattern pieces up to yourself to check the length.

If you want your dress longer, now is the time to make the patterns longer (page 29).

If you want your dress shorter, it's easier to do that now too (page 29)!

(2) Choose a collar pattern (on pullout page P4). Trace the pattern onto your pattern paper and cut it out.

(3) Pin the collar pattern to the felt, trace it, and cut it out.

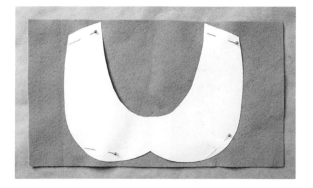

Dress Fabrics

For this project I used a light- to medium-weight cotton for the dress. If you are a more experienced stitcher or are working on the dress with an adult who sews, you can choose a fancier material such as satin or velvet. Keep your fabric choice simple the first time, but I encourage you to experiment with textured materials for the next one.

(4) Fold the dress fabric in half lengthwise, matching up the selvages. (Normally, you fold the fabric right sides together. Here, it's folded the other way so it is easier to see. Both will work for this dress.) Pin the dress front pattern on top, lining the straight edge up with the fold. Pin the back pattern piece on top, too. If your fabric has a print with a definite direction, make sure the front and back are in the same direction. You may need more fabric if this is the case.

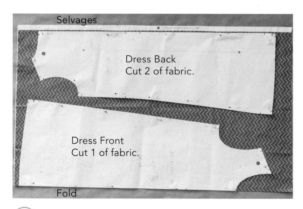

Selvages

Dress Back
Cut 2 of fabric.

Dress Front
Cut 1 of fabric.

Fold

(5) Trace the patterns onto your fabric. Cut them out through both layers. You will have 3 pieces—1 front and 2 backs.

LET'S CREATE!

Sew with a ⅝˝ seam allowance unless the instructions say otherwise. Backstitch at the beginning and end of all seams. Press the seam allowances open after each seam.

Use a matching zipper and thread. (I used different colors here just so you can easily see them.)

Putting in the Zipper

If you've never put in an invisible zipper, read Zippers (page 38) and practice on the Simple Zipper Pouch (page 38).

(1) Grab an adult to help with the iron. Set the iron to low heat and iron the teeth of your zipper as flat as possible.

Caution! Hot!

(2) Lay the 2 back pieces next to each other, right sides up. Line them up at the neck along the straight sides at the center back (CB) mark. Open the zipper and lay it facedown on the right-hand back piece like in the photo, about ¼˝ from the edge. The zipper pull should be facing the fabric. Line it up with the zipper marks and pin it in place. (The dress and the zipper should be right sides together.)

Center back

Zipper right side down

3 Put the zipper foot on your machine. Put the pinned piece under the zipper foot, with the fabric right side up and the foot just to the left of the teeth.

Sew as close as possible to the teeth as far as you can until the zipper pull gets in the way.

4 Lay the back piece you just sewed on top of the other back piece, right sides together. Line the loose zipper tape up with the center back of the other back piece the same as in Step 2 and pin the zipper in place, about ¼˝ from the cut edge.

5 Repeat Step 3 to sew the side of the zipper you just pinned.

6 Thread a hand-sewing needle and hand stitch where your machine was unable to sew using a backstitch (page 16).

That's it! You've put in an invisible zipper.

Sewing the Dress

(1) Put the regular presser foot back on the sewing machine.

Pin the dress back pieces right sides together from the end of the zipper to the bottom of the dress, matching the notches.

(2) Sew the center back seam from the end of the zipper to the bottom of the dress.

(3) Match up the dress front and back at the shoulders, right sides together, using the notches. Pin and sew the shoulders together.

(4) Match the front and back along the side seams, right sides together. Pin and sew from the armholes down.

FLAT SEAMS

Press all your seams flat after sewing for neater, more accurate results that lie better against your body. Usually, seams in clothing are pressed open, but sometimes they can't be, like with zippers, hems, or casings. Generally, I press to one side.

LET'S FINISH

Neck and Arms

(1) On the wrong side of the dress, draw a line with your fabric marker ¾″ in from the edge of the neck on the dress. Do the same thing on each armhole.

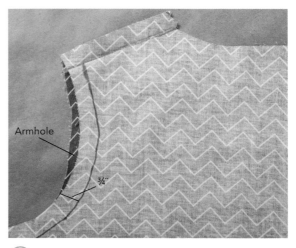

(2) To help make finishing the armholes easier, change your machine stitch length to between 4 and 5, which is an extra-long or basting stitch. Sew around the neckline and armholes on the lines you just drew.

(3) Carefully snip little slits into the seam allowance along *just* the neck and armhole curves. Careful! Don't cut into your stitches.

(4) Turn the dress right side out. Fold the raw edges at the neck and armholes over to the wrong side of the fabric along the stitching; pin. You can iron the fold before pinning to help keep it in place. The slits will help the fabric spread out and sit flat around the curves.

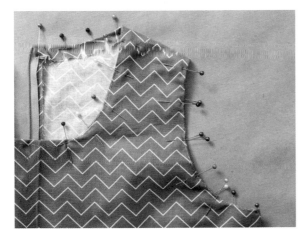

(5) Topstitch around the neckline and armholes close to the folded edge. Use the edge of the presser foot to keep your stitching even. Use the seam ripper to carefully remove the big stitches that helped you turn the edges under.

(6) Try on the dress and mark how short you would like it. See How to Hem (page 35) to hem it.

Necklace

(1) Let's make the "necklace." Grab the collar you cut out when you first started, along with your rhinestones and glue gun or needle and thread.

(2) Lay out the rhinestones on the collar in your own design. Refer back to the inspiration drawing you worked on earlier (page 111). Try out as many different designs as you like.

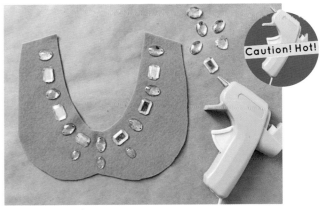

Caution! Hot!

GOT A CELL PHONE?

Take pictures of your different designs. It makes it easier to redo an earlier one that turns out to be your favorite. And it also gives you ideas for your next collar design!

(3) Glue or hand sew the rhinestones in place.

4 Cut the ribbon into 2 equal pieces. Pin and sew 1 piece to each end of the collar.

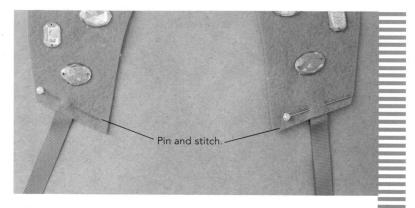

Pin and stitch.

5 Try the collar on with the dress. Tie the ribbons in the back so that everything lies flat and falls in the right place. Trim the ribbons shorter if you want.

Style It!

★ The best part of this dress is that you have the option to create two dresses! Since the "necklaces" are removable, you can make a second one with an entirely different look.

★ Instead of the rhinestones, cut out different shapes of felt or fabric to match and make your own design. Try cutting circles of different colors and sizes and layering them on top of each other, or pick your favorite fabric that complements your dress and make the collar out of that. You can even wear these necklace collars with a plain T-shirt or top.

Party Purse

WHAT YOU NEED

★ ⅓ yard of medium- to heavyweight cotton, or a specialty material like glitter vinyl, faux leather, or suede for the outside of the purse (Because you will fold the fabric to shape the purse, avoid picking a design that won't look right if it's turned upside down.)

★ ⅓ yard of lightweight fabric for the lining

★ ⅓ yard of stiff, medium-weight fusible interfacing (such as Pellon Craft-Fuse) (*optional*)

★ ⅔–1 yard of 2″-wide ribbon for the strap

★ Magnetic snap closure, sew-on snap, or hook-and-loop tape

★ Basic sewing supplies

★ Pattern paper

LET'S PREP

(1) If you are using inter-facing, follow the directions on the interfacing to fuse it to the wrong side of your lining fabric. Be careful when using a hot iron and ask an adult for help if you need it.

(2) Draw a 10″ × 16″ rectangle on paper for the purse pattern. If you have lots of experience, you can draw this shape directly on your fabrics.

(3) Pin, trace, and cut out 1 rectangle each from the lining and the outside fabric.

(4) Measure yourself to decide how long you would like the purse strap to be. Add 2″ to that number. Cut 1 piece of ribbon to that length.

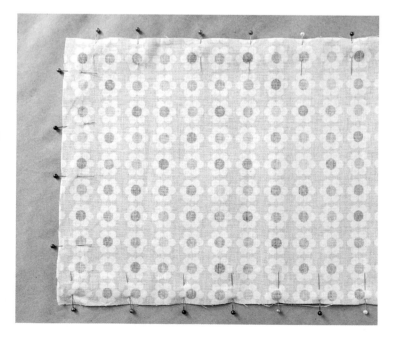

FANCY FABRIC TIPS

★ If you choose to use some faux leather, suede, or other specialty material as lining, use a pressing cloth when you iron the interfacing. Do a test on a scrap piece to make sure it works and follow the product instructions.

★ Pinholes won't go away in some of these fancy fabrics. Place your pins inside the seam allowance area so the holes won't be seen. If the fabric is hard to pin through, use small binder clips (page 121).

★ Use the proper needle in your sewing machine. Some materials require a special needle when sewing. A universal needle usually works fine, but it's more likely to break than a needle made for the specific material. Get some help from an adult if you need to.

LET'S CREATE!

Sew with a ½″ seam allowance unless the instructions say otherwise. Backstitch at the beginning and end of all seams. Press the seam allowances open after each seam; some specialty fabrics can just be pressed flat with your finger, not an iron.

(1) Match up the lining and outside rectangles, right sides together. Pin along both long sides and 1 short side.

2 Sew down 1 long side, across the short side (this will be the flap on the outside of your purse), and up the other long side.

3 Cut off at an angle the corners you just sewed.

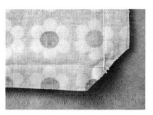

4 Turn the purse right side out through the opening at the top and push the corners out so they are square. Use a chopstick or something else pointy.

5 Fold the open edges of the purse in ¾˝ to the wrong side.

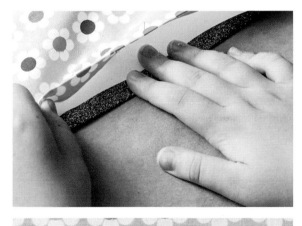

6 Pin closed. Sew along the pinned edge.

7 Fold up the end of the rectangle that you just sewed 5½˝, so that the lining sides are together.

Fold up.

8 Sandwich the cut ends of the ribbon 1˝ in between the front and back of the purse on both sides. Make sure the strap is not twisted. Pin (or clip) along the short sides.

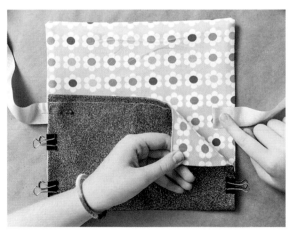

9 Sew the sides of the purse closed where you've pinned using the edge of the presser foot as a guide to stay straight.

Style It!

★ Make your purse even more party ready with extra sparkle. Use some rhinestones like the ones you used for your necklace dress and add a design to the front of your purse. Glue the stones in place.

★ Hand sew a fun sparkly chain to the purse as the strap.

LET'S FINISH

1 Fold down the rest of the rectangle to make the front flap. Mark a spot on the front of the purse underneath the flap for the closure. Mark the same spot on the wrong (lining) side of the flap.

2 If you are using a magnetic snap closure, follow the instructions that came with it to put it on.

If you have a regular snap, sew it on by hand. If you have hook-and-loop tape, sew it on by machine.

3 Cover up where the closure is on the right side of the flap by making a bow (see Glitter Headband, Let's Finish, Steps 1–4, page 124) from extra fabric or ribbon. You could also use a sparkly button. Glue or hand sew it to the front of the flap.

Done!

Glitter Headband

WHAT YOU NEED

★ Flat headband, ½″–2″ wide

★ Glitter ribbon, as wide as or a little wider than the headband

★ Double-stick foam tape*

★ Scissors

★ Glue gun or glue stick

If you do not have double-stick tape, you can also use a glue gun following the same steps.

LET'S PREP

(1) Measure your headband and cut a piece of the double-stick tape the same length. If your double-stick tape is wider than the headband, trim it to match.

(2) Add 1″ to the headband measurement. Cut 1 piece of ribbon this length.

LET'S CREATE!

(1) Starting at an end of your headband, peel the paper off 1 side of the double-stick tape and stick it onto the headband. Try to keep it as even and centered as possible. Press down well to make sure it stays.

(2) Peel the paper off the top of the double-stick tape. Again, start at an end of the headband. Fold the first ½″ of ribbon under an end of the headband. Line up the ribbon on the tape. Carefully stick the ribbon onto the headband, making sure it is smooth and centered as you go.

(3) Fold the extra ribbon under the other end of the headband. Glue both ribbon ends to the underside of the headband.

LET'S FINISH

(1) Cut 1 piece of ribbon 3″ long. Cut another piece of ribbon twice as long as the ribbon is wide. Cut 3 small pieces of double-stick tape.

(2) Stick 1 small piece of double-stick tape in the middle of the wrong side of the 3″ piece of ribbon. Peel the paper off the top.

(3) Fold the ends of the ribbon in to the middle and press in place.

(4) Wrap the other piece of ribbon around the center of the bow loops and use another piece of double-stick tape to hold it in place.

(5) Use the last small piece of tape to fasten the ribbon to your headband wherever you would like.

Glam Shoe Clips

WHAT YOU NEED

★ Alligator hair clips

★ ⅛ yard of heavyweight bold or glitter fabric, or vinyl or faux leather

★ Felt scraps to match your fabric

★ Glue gun

LET'S PREP

(1) See Tracing and Templates (page 29) to make 1 template for the shoe clip pattern on pullout page P4 you want to use—the heart or the circle. Then trace and cut 2 of that shape from felt and 2 from fabric.

(2) Cut out 2 pieces of felt about 1½″ × 1½″.

DESIGN YOUR OWN

You can design your own shape for the shoe clips, you know. Just draw the design you want on some copy paper, cut it out, and trace it onto your felt and fabric.

LET'S CREATE!

(1) Glue the felt shapes to the wrong sides of the fabric shapes.

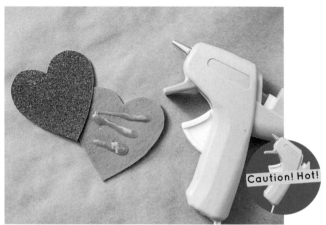

Caution! Hot!

(2) Put a line of glue straight down the center of the felt side of the shape. Press the flat side of the alligator clip down on the glue. Make sure not to glue the clip shut.

3 Stick the small felt square between the "jaws" of the clip so you cover any teeth. Glue the edges of the felt square down.

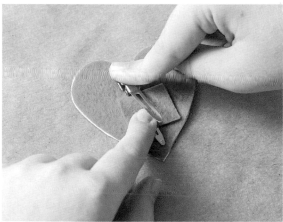

4 Repeat Steps 2 and 3 to finish the other shoe clip.

LET'S FINISH

Let dry and then try them on your shoes.

Make More Shoe Clips

Match a clip to your Necklace Dress (page 112); use the same fabric and add a rhinestone in the center.

Make flowers just like the ones on the Flirty Floral Cardigan (page 54), and glue alligator clips onto the back of them.

Create felt or ribbon bows (see Glitter Headband, page 123), attach them to felt squares, and glue alligator clips to the back.

ABOUT THE AUTHOR

Rachel lives in New York City with her dog, Molly.

Rachel Low's mission is to make sewing and crafting simple, stylish, and fun. Rachel has always loved exploring her creativity. In particular, she loves to sew, embroider, and craft, all of which she learned from her mother.

When she grew up, she worked in the corporate world. It was exciting. She worked with incredibly creative people, got to wear sophisticated clothes, and traveled all over Europe and Asia. She explored museums, flea markets, and many unique shopping areas around the world. That made Rachel more passionate about arts and design.

When she got the chance to change careers, she decided to do what she loved—sewing and crafting. That's how she came to open Pins & Needles, a modern sewing and crafting boutique and studio. After opening the shop she discovered that her community of like-minded creative people included a new generation of girls who wanted to make beautiful things, too.

Rachel says the best part of her job is guiding and teaching the young girls who take classes with her. She is thrilled to have the opportunity to nurture them. It led her to write this book to reach more future designers, artists, makers, and style icons. She wants to encourage girls to create, have fun, and feel good about what they can do and what they can make. Time and time again, Rachel hears from parents that she has given a tremendous gift to so many girls. What could be better?

RESOURCES

My favorite places to get assorted sewing, craft, and DIY supplies:

Pins & Needles • pinsandneedlesnyc.com

Create for Less • createforless.com

Etsy for various craft supplies • etsy.com

Fabric.com

Michaels • michaels.com

Jo-Ann Fabrics • joann.com

Where to look at fabulous fabrics (not all these websites sell their products online, but you can window-shop):

Michael Miller Fabrics • michaelmillerfabrics.com

Robert Kaufman Fabrics • robertkaufmanfabrics.com

Riley Blake Fabrics • rileyblakefabrics.com

Alexander Henry • ahfabrics.com

Spandexworld • spandexworld.com

National Nonwovens • woolfelt.com

Spoonflower • spoonflower.com